Money & Marriage

How to Choose a Financially Compatible Spouse

By Michael Sion

AMERICAN INSTITUTE *for* ECONOMIC RESEARCH

Great Barrington, MA

Money & Marriage:
How to Choose a Financially Compatible Spouse
Economic Bulletin, Vol. L No. 12 December 2010

Published by:
American Institute for Economic Research
Economic Bulletin
250 Division Street
PO Box 1000
Great Barrington, MA 01230
888-528-1216
info@aier.org
www.aier.org

Economic Bulletin (ISSN 0424–2769) (USPS 167–360) is published once a month at Great Barrington, Massachusetts, by American Institute for Economic Research, a scientific and educational organization with no stockholders, chartered under Chapter 180 of the General Laws of Massachusetts. Periodical postage paid at Great Barrington, Massachusetts. Printed in the United States of America. Subscription: $59 per year. POSTMASTER: Send address changes to *Economic Bulletin*, American Institute for Economic Research, Great Barrington, Massachusetts 01230.

Book Design and Production: Jonathan Sylbert

ISBN 13: 978-091361077-0
Printed in U.S.A.

Disclaimer
Neither the author nor publisher is providing legal, investment, tax or accounting advice. The author and publisher specifically disclaim any liability resulting from the use or application of the information in this book. The reader should seek the services of a qualified professional for all legal, investment, tax or accounting advice.

Contents

> "When you make a lifetime commitment, be sure you know how you're going to pay the bills."
> —George Kinder

Introduction

IT IS common knowledge that one in two marriages in our country end in divorce. Indeed, approximately 2.2 million marriages take place in the United States each year—and slightly more than half of these legally tied knots end up undone, according to the National Center for Health Statistics.

In the litany of reasons why couples who enter matrimony subsequently enter legal proceedings to dissolve their unions, one frequently cited by experts as the No. 1 conflict in marriage is discord over money-related issues. For an unfortunately large number of couples, the phrase, "'Til death do us part," in the standard marriage vow might as well be, "'Til debt do us part."

Most partners who decide to become husband and wife spend little to no time discussing how they will combine their finances after they wed. "When the pixie dust is on, you tend to downplay the role of money in your relationship," says Kevin Roth, a licensed marriage and family therapist based in Philadelphia whose areas of expertise include couples communication and conflict resolution. "Couples can say, 'When we get married, it won't matter.' But after a year it will surface. Or it will surface right away."

Lee Slater, a New York-based certified financial planner and certified divorce financial analyst and a past president of the Association of Divorce Financial Planners, confirms this view: "Too many people just ignore the financial considerations and deal with their sexual needs and emotional feelings. When you talk to therapists, they'll tell you that people are really happy to be talking about their feelings and the most intimate sexual details of their lives. But money is the last thing that people want to talk about in therapy. It's just the way we're brought up. How often do people sit around in a family and talk about spending and saving and financial family goals?"

1

"I am always surprised when couples tell me they didn't consider money as an important aspect to think about or talk about before marriage," adds marriage and family therapist Kristy Archuleta, who specializes on issues surrounding money and finances and teaches personal financial planning as a professor at Kansas State University. "Couples say they just didn't realize how big of an issue it would be."

But a big issue it is. A 2008 study by researchers at three U.S. universities that involved 100 wives and 100 husbands found that couples don't necessarily fight *most* about money, but conflicts about money tend to be the most intense and the most left unresolved. "Definitely not enough couples talk about money—and if they do talk about it, they don't talk about in the depth that they need to," Archuleta says.

> Almost no couples really consider financial compatibility before they get married. Too many people just ignore the financial considerations and deal with their sexual needs and emotional feelings.
> — Lee Slater, divorce financial analyst

A 2006 *USA Today/CNN/Gallup* poll found that nearly two-thirds of couples who responded to the survey did little or no talking about this topic pre-marriage. The poll also found that the financial issues causing the most frequent strife in a marriage are spending too much and saving too little. The high divorce rate and the fact that monetary issues are a leading (if not *the* leading) cause of failed marriages point to the need for a guide like this one that helps a person assess financial compatibility with his/her partner before the two become legally bound.

In Marriage, a Money Match Matters

Marriage, like owning a home, is an investment. Unfortunately, "Love is blind"—or at least has the power to impede people's vision. This may be especially true for younger people. Data from the National Center for Health Statistics show that in the U.S., nearly 37 percent of women and 39 percent of men between ages 20 and 24 who marry will end up divorced. In the age 25 to 29 group, 16 percent of women and 22 percent of men who tie the knot will sever it. (The numbers continue to decline after that. For example, in the age 30 to 34 range, 8.5 percent of women and 11.5 percent of men will end up divorced.)

This book is essential reading, particularly for people in their 20's who are considering marriage and are ready to take a hard, serious look at their own and their partner's financial state and attitude toward money and thus determine whether their legal union will literally prosper or fail. The chapters address whether a person is fiscally ready for marriage, whether the person's partner is fiscally ready—and whether the two should proceed with investing their futures together. Strategies for keeping the marital boat financially afloat are explained as well.

Marriage Is Like a Business

A marriage is akin to a business partnership. The toll that a failed marriage exacts includes more than emotional damage for the partners (as well as any dependants). It also includes financial damage. In contrast, two spouses cohabitating in a mutually beneficial relationship and pursuing sensible financial goals enjoy a formula for long-term happiness and prosperity.

Clear communication about money—and creating a financial scenario each partner is comfortable with—is critical to sustaining a good marriage, says financial planner Slater. "You must talk about it in advance and come to some understanding of how you're going to live your financial lives."

When two partners work together to determine how they will generate income and how they'll budget and invest, they can weather inevitable financial storms such as a drop in income, a bad investment, a job loss, or unexpected medical expenses. "When something goes wrong, they know immediately it'll be a source of a problem, and they adapt, rather than waiting until credit-card companies start calling and they don't have the money to pay," Slater says. "They're not going to let the current economic crisis destroy their marriage."

See if You're a 'Money Match'

This book is not a financial primer. But it *is* a primer for determining if you and your partner are financially compatible. Ignore the following 16 chapters at your own peril.

A good, solid marriage contributes to a full, rich life. If it were possible simply to "live on love," that would be well and fine. But in the real world, people must live on money, too. Marriages constantly take work, and so do financial affairs.

It's vital to take intelligent steps *before* getting married to review your personal affairs and that of your partner. Having serious discussions to determine if you are financially compatible and capable of working together toward shared goals—in short, that you are "a money match"—is a mark of partners mature enough to marry.

Such prudence can prove rewarding by helping a person choose the right partner—and avoid the kind who would prove to be an extremely costly mistake.

> "He who marries for love without money has
> good nights and sorry days."
> —Anonymous

1

Determining Your Money Personality

EACH OF us carries all kinds of emotional baggage—whether fears sustained from childhood, bruised feelings from past friendships or romances, frustrated career dreams, and so on. Similarly, each of us harbors deep-seated beliefs and habits born of positive experiences. These memories influence our relationships—including how we handle money.

From our parents or circumstances growing up, we develop money personalities. In general, some of us are spenders, and some of us are savers—with gradations in behavior spanning the spectrum.

If you want a healthy relationship with a marital partner, you will need to get in sync with this person when it comes to your financial life together. You will need to understand this person's money personality. That's the subject of this chapter, which is designed for both you and your partner to read, and to compare results. They should prove interesting.

It may very well turn out that you and your partner lack and will not be able to achieve financial compatibility. Perhaps one of you is an incurable spender and the other an inveterate saver. You are destined to butt heads over and over because your values are just too different. Or perhaps each of you is a spender, and neither is able to adjust his or her behavior and guide the other onto a path of fiscal responsibility. You will end up pointing fingers at each other for amassing debt. Or, in an opposite scenario, perhaps each of you is an uncontrollable saver, loath to part with even a spare cent. You could end up blaming each other for never being able to slow down, lighten up, and smell the roses.

Better to discover your money personalities before you get married so you can intelligently decide if you can merge your traits in a productive manner and are willing to do so . . . or if it's better for the two of you to invest time in finding more suitable partners.

The assessment can begin right now.

Your Money Personality

Many books and magazine articles have been written concerning how to determine your "money personality" (also called your "financial personality" or "money type"). Most of these personality categories are versions or combinations of the spender and the saver. Authors vary on the number of money personalities. Some list five; others categorize eight or nine. Most people probably are combinations of several of the personality types, but can identify most closely with one of the types.

Financial planner Lee Slater outlines five general categories of money personalities.

The Puppy Dog

Also known as *The Spender*, Puppy Dogs crave immediate gratification and get it from spending money. It doesn't matter if they are purchasing items for themselves, buying gifts for others, or going out to eat. They want it now. "They're like kids," Slater says. "Picture a child in a supermarket spotting the coin machine that dispenses little toys and begging a parent for quarters. Puppy Dogs can get hooked on the Home Shopping Network sitting in front of their TVs, or on eBay stuck in front of their computers, bidding on items going on sale."

Some Puppy Dogs, predominantly women, are addicted to clothes. They roam the big department stores or the small boutiques, shopping for the sake of shopping. Male Puppy Dogs can be the guys who are always eating out in restaurants, hanging out in bars, partying, or taking women out on flashy dates. A subcategory of the Puppy Dog is the spender who equates money with power and respect, such as the high roller who always picks up the tab for friends at the restaurant or drives a flashy sport car even though the vehicle is financed at 100 percent.

Sometimes Puppy Dogs are people who find themselves with more money to spend than they've ever had before, yet have never learned the value of a dollar. A typical example, Slater says, is the young guy in the financial industry, just out of college. He's earning his first good salary and expects to be making huge bucks in the near future, so he's spending like he doesn't have to worry about tomorrow. "He feels like he's been waiting to do this all his life, and now he's living the dream," Slater says.

But Puppy Dogs can be older professionals, too. "I did a divorce analysis of a guy who was a big-time bank- er with Lehman Brothers, making $1 million a year, and he and his wife still didn't have money left over," Slater says. "He was spending a lot of money on bodybuilding and supplements. And

> The tendency is to think it's all about find- ing the right person. But even if you find the perfect match, eventually you're going to have problems. Here's what you want to ask your- self: "Is this person flexible and willing to work with me? And am I willing to work with this person?"
>
> — Kevin Roth, marriage and family therapist

after the breakup, his new girlfriend was spending his money like crazy."

The consummate Puppy Dog? "Michael Jackson," Slater says. "He made a huge fortune in his lifetime, but whatever money he had, he found a way to spend it, and he died with a reported $400 million in unpaid debt."

The Squirrel

Also known as *The Saver*, Squirrels like having money in the bank and get gratification from seeing the account build up. They focus strongly on specific financial goals. It's hard for Squirrels to spend money because they just put it away—saving for a house, saving to pay off credit cards, or saving to pay off college funds.

"Squirrels typically are the opposites of Puppy Dogs because they're will- ing to wait as long as necessary to have the things they want," Slater says. "I know Squirrels who don't make a lot of money, but really want to buy a house or get into a really great apartment, and they're willing to live pretty meager lives as they save up. They bring their lunch to work and never eat out unless it's fast food, or they have a two-for-$20 deal at a chain restaurant, and then they never buy drinks or appetizers. Squirrels plan their purchases. If they buy a television or computer, they are content to hold off until there's a sale. Squirrels are good Wal-Mart customers. They think twice before buying branded products."

Squirrels hate seeing credit-card bills coming in the mail. They not only dislike carrying a big mortgage, they are bothered by having *any* mortgage and dream of paying it all off. They generally see the world as having limited possibilities and feel they need to hang on to what they have.

The Ostrich

Also known as *The Avoider*, when it comes to financial responsibilities, Ostriches stick their heads in the sand. These are the people who let the bills stack up. If they invest, they put all their money into money markets because they don't get around to investing in mutual funds or other securities that require research. They're not in denial; they just willfully avoid financial issues.

"I have a big tax practice," Slater says. "My Ostriches typically don't do their taxes until they're three years behind, and the IRS sends them a letter. All of a sudden, they come in to do that and bring multiple years of paperwork. I've learned that there's just no way I can prompt them to file on time. I can send them reminder letters and call them to come in, and they just don't do it. You can't change them. They won't change for whatever reason. When they get their taxes done, they feel like a huge burden has been lifted from them. Then the next year, they don't come in again."

The Sparrow

Also known as *The Money Monk*, Sparrows believe in the simple life and don't like spending money. They're not necessarily saving for anything, they just believe they don't need much. "Monks are the perfect example," Slater says. "They live that very simple life, free of earthly possessions. Nourishing their soul is what really counts. Sparrows take it to the level of really not believing it's right to have stuff. They believe that unnecessary consumption is bad. They don't need to go on vacations. They can just stay home. They don't need a 50-inch plasma television; if they want a TV, they can still get by on an old 30-inch model."

Sparrows don't like leaving a large carbon footprint. Sparrows typically are gainfully employed, but not in jobs that pay a large income. Sparrows aren't corporate executives or professionals with graduate degrees, such as physicians or lawyers or engineers. Sparrows may be teachers, government workers, health-food store clerks, nonprofit-agency employees, or self-described starving artists.

The Owl

Also known as *The Money Guru*, Owls are the most financially mature of the money personalities. They think a lot about money. They have money smarts. They want to save for important goals. But unlike Squirrels, Owls' main focus isn't saving, it's money management. They monitor their investments. They keep their income and expenditures in sync.

"They're the people who call up in February to make their March tax appointment, and their records are organized, they have spreadsheets," Slater says. "Owls never fail to make at least the minimum credit-card payment. They might have a nice house, but they probably don't have the most expensive furniture in the world. Instead of buying a $10,000 couch, they buy the $2,500 couch. They drive a car that might be a Honda Accord—which is cheap to run, never breaks down, and has the best resale value—instead of driving a luxury car like a Mercedes 550, which might end up costing double the cost of a Honda Accord after three or four years of ownership."

The Money Match Matrix

From the previous descriptions you've probably determined which money personality you and your partner are. (And if you're still not sure, questions in Chapter 2 may help you decide.) That chart below is a quick, easy way to assess potential good or poor money matches. "B" stands for bliss; "M" for match, as in a good match; "R" is for risky; and "D" is disaster.

	Owl	Squirrel	Puppy Dog	Ostrich	Sparrow
Owl	B	B	M	M	M
Squirrel	B	M	R	R	M
Puppy Dog	M	R	D	D	D
Ostrich	M	R	D	D	D
Sparrow	M	M	D	D	M

These aren't absolute terms. Flexibility—the willingness of each partner to work with the other toward a mutually beneficial outcome—is even more important to achieving financial compatibility than individual money personalities. "Just about everyone has personality traits falling into several categories," says marriage and family therapist Kevin Roth.

"One or more traits may be dominant. The key to a healthy relationship is *flexibility*. If you or your partner lacks flexibility and is locked into one personality type most of the time, and you're partnered with someone who is rigidly another type, such as a Puppy Dog with a Sparrow, you can probably predict the dynamic that's going to show up. There will be conflict over one partner's acquisitions and the other's dislike of acquisitions, and it might turn pretty ugly."

Stress, such as financial woes, causes rigidity. If one of you loses a job, or if unexpected, hefty bills show up, your true colors can emerge.

"The tendency in discussing ideal mates is to think it's all about finding the right person, and if you find the right person, that's it," Roth says. "But whoever you marry is going to bring up your issues. Even if you find the perfect match, eventually you're going to have problems. Here's what you want to ask yourself about a partner: 'Is this person I'm with flexible and willing to work with me? And am I willing to work with this person?'"

Flexibility can make some otherwise poor matches succeed. Nevertheless, some combinations seem more chemically volatile than others.

Owls Match the Most

Owls most often hook up with fellow Owls, and this is a blissful match, but Owls can match with all the rest, if the Owl or the partner is willing to be flexible. An Owl and a Squirrel can match, but the Squirrel must accept the Owl's willingness to spend money. An Owl can match with a Puppy Dog, but the Owl must be able to keep the Puppy Dog's spending from sabotaging financial obligations and must adapt to the Puppy Dog's behavior. The Puppy Dog must accept the Owl's position. In an Owl and Ostrich match, the Owl must take charge of paying bills, filing taxes, and investing. The Ostrich must accept the Owl's position. Another good match for the Owl is with a Sparrow. The Sparrow may not put much stock in material comforts, but doesn't complain if they appear as blessings.

Squirrel's Are Next Best

Two Squirrels make a good match, but if one suddenly has a change of heart, perhaps triggered by a midlife crisis, and now wants to start enjoying finer material goods, or travel more, he or she may blame the other for being too stingy and having deprived their lives of enjoyment. A Squirrel and a Puppy Dog is a risky match. They'll probably be at each other's throats all the time. However, if they develop good communication, each can benefit the other—the Squirrel keeping the Puppy Dog's spending in check, the Puppy Dog helping the Squirrel loosen up and enjoy life more. Otherwise, their relationship is doomed.

Also risky is a Squirrel and an Ostrich. The Squirrel can make sure the bills are paid, but may grow very upset with the Ostrich's lack of fiscal responsibility. The Ostrich must respect the Squirrel's values and not resent the Squirrel's reluctance to spend even if money seems available. A better match is a Squirrel with a Sparrow. The Sparrow doesn't need much to live on; the Squirrel is willing to wait until cash is in hand to make a big financial move.

The Problem Puppy Dog

Puppy Dogs are hard to match. A Puppy Dog matched with a Puppy Dog is a disaster waiting to happen. At least one of them will have to learn, somehow, to be fiscally responsible. Not much better is the match between a Puppy Dog and an Ostrich. The Puppy Dog sees the money draining away, but the Ostrich pays it no mind, as if it doesn't matter. They will have to learn, somehow, to be fiscally responsible. A Puppy Dog and a Sparrow is another disastrous match. They'll find it nearly impossible to negotiate a middle ground. The Sparrow will find it difficult to have all those possessions the Puppy Dog accumulates.

The Ostrich and the Sparrow

The Ostrich is as much a challenge as the Puppy Dog. Both are more likely to find success matched to an Owl. An Ostrich matched with another Ostrich, a Puppy Dog, or Sparrow can be a disaster. The Ostrich neglects money issues; the Puppy Dog spends and ignores; the Sparrow may tend to avoid dealing with money issues, too. Sparrows, on the other hand, can match up with Owls, Squirrels, or even another Sparrow, as long as both Sparrows are careful about maintaining income and a reserve of savings, and never grow tired of their Spartan lifestyle.

After figuring out your and your partner's money personalities, you each should think deeply about how financially compatible you are, and what steps each of you will need to take to make your marriage one that stays financially afloat and is sailing on a course toward financial security.

Taking a close look at each other's financial situation—getting down to actual dollars and cents—is the subject of Chapter 2.

One Couple's Story

Like most couples, Milan and Monica didn't talk much about money before they married. But each did take mental note of the other's financial situation.

Milan, who was 30 and previously married to a Puppy Dog, admired Monica's thriving business as an art director: "That she was a successful career woman definitely made a huge difference." Monica, 34 at the time, saw that Milan, a graphic artist and website designer, was gainfully employed and very creative and skilled. "I did not have any concerns that he would not be financially OK," she says.

What has sustained them for eight years as husband and wife are not only emotional and physical connections, but the financial compatibility from being Owls. When important financial matters come up, the Owls work toward the same goals and their wedding is an example.

Monica didn't want an expensive gown. Neither partner likes diamonds, so the engagement and wedding rings were white gold—total cost, about $1,000. The ceremony and reception were at a friend's house. One hundred people were invited. The couple rented tables and other essentials. The big-ticket item was $4,000 for food. The remaining toll: $1,000. The couple took a mini-honeymoon at nearby Lake Tahoe, Nev., which cost less than $1,000, and saved for a longer honeymoon to Tuscany.

When it comes to household finances, the two share bill-paying duties. "I still have my old bank account I use to pay the TV bill and groceries," Milan says. "We have a joint account, and Monica writes checks for the sewer and water bills, and the mortgage and power bill are automated. I pay for my own health care because it would be more expensive to add me to the plan covering her and our son.

"We pay off our credit card pretty quickly. We don't buy something nice if we don't have the money. The only debt we have is for things that are unforeseeable, like medical bills."

While money issues constitute the No. 1 source of conflict in most marriages, Milan says parenting their 2-year-old son triggers more discussions.

"The No. 1 challenge for us is staying honest when we communicate about family matters," says Monica, who became a stay-at-home mother after their son was born while Milan runs his advertising art and web-design business. "We talk about money daily because when you have your own business, money isn't always consistent," she says. "You don't have a budget. You do what you can with what you get. You try to plan as best as you can. We do talk pretty openly and candidly and know where we are financially and equally. I know exactly how much we have. It's not a conflict. We keep it honest and real."

"Don't tell me where your priorities are. Show me where you spend your money and I'll tell you what they are."

—James W. Frick

2

Assessing Your and Your Partner's Financial Situation

SO WE know that there's a lot more to the formula for a successful marriage than "chemistry." After all, there's much more to a marriage than an initial romantic connection. As couples discover, financial pressures can have a fizzling effect on what had been fireworks.

In this chapter we'll take a close look at actual dollars and cents—yours and your partner's. We'll look at what each of you has now and has had in the past in the way of assets and debts. We'll also look at what you plan to have in the future. Finally, we'll have each of you write out a short goal statement.

(After reviewing your respective financial status and goals, you may change your mind about which money personality best describes you. Refer back to Chapter 1.)

The way your partner handles money reveals a great deal about his or her values, including honesty, responsibility, discipline, and decision making. By reviewing your and your partner's financial histories, you can discover a great deal about each other's true nature. Are you selfish or cooperative? Willing to share or even sacrifice instead of fulfilling immediate gratification? Able to plan ahead instead of living for the moment? Have you or your partner ever filed for bankruptcy? What are your credit scores? What assets and debts does each of you possess? What are your respective incomes and work histories?

These are critical pieces of information that help form the jigsaw puzzle that will give you a clear picture of your partner's character. This is vital to the health of your marriage because you will only be able to resolve discord over money matters if you are able to work toward common objectives.

Your Financial Situation

It can take a measure of will to sit down and figure out your financial status. But it is well worth your time. What's more, it's the fair and right thing to do so that you can give your partner an accurate picture of your financial health. Answering the questions in the following table will provide a clear picture.

What is your . . .	You	Your Partner	Total
sum of liquid assets[1]			
sum of investments other than in retirement funds			
sum of investments in retirement funds			
average monthly income			
credit score[2]			
total debt			
debt in credit cards			
debt in car loans, student loans, or other large loans			
debt due to creditors in a large judgment			
debt in a mortgage			
amount of debt you're paying down each month			

[1] Liquid assets include cash or assets that can be converted quickly into cash, such as savings in a bank account.
[2] This can be obtained online, for a fee, at various websites.

Your Financial Goal Statement

Now we're going to have a little fun. The following questions will help you focus on where you're heading in your financial life. If you're in your 20's or 30's, these questions may seem irrelevant to you at this very moment, but you must project yourself into the future. If you're mature enough to get married, these questions are pertinent.

Each of you should take a sheet of paper and answer the following questions.

This is a preliminary step to each of you writing a goal statement.

1. How do you intend to retire your debts?
2. What is your deadline for paying off each debt?
3. Do you wish to buy a house or condominium, or rent?
4. What big-ticket items do you wish to own?
5. How do you intend to invest financially after you're married?
6. How many children do you intend to have?
7. At what age do you wish to retire?
8. What lifestyle do you envision for your retirement?

Now that you're focused on some of the specifics of the near and distant futures you want for yourself, it's time for each of you to write down your respective financial goal statement. This statement need not fill up an entire sheet of paper. It can be as short as a paragraph—or as lengthy as you want.

A few pointers:

- Write a few short sentences that reflect your current financial situation.
- Break down your goals into short-term, medium-term, and long-term. (You might devote a sentence or a paragraph to each type.)
- Goals should reflect *your* values and dreams, not someone else's expectations for you.
- Consider S.M.A.R.T. goals. This acronym stands for "specific, measurable, attainable, realistic, and timely." For example, saying "I want to be rich" is an unspecific goal. Writing, "I want $100,000 in the bank" *is* specific and measurable. This goal should also be attainable. In other words, do you or will you have sources of income that allow you to amass the $100,000? Also, state *how* you will attain the goal, such as "I will set aside $1,000 a month in interest-bearing certificates of deposit until I have $100,000 in the account." A S.M.A.R.T. goal is also realistic. Be honest with yourself. Is $100,000 too high a figure or too low? An example of an unrealistic goal is, "I will write a novel and make at least $100,000 from it." The realistic goal is finishing a novel and getting it published. That is something over which you have realistic control. And finally, give your goal a time frame: "I want $100,000 in the bank within eight years."

Justin's Goal Statement

"I'm 27 and living within my means in a modest apartment, but I have big plans. I have $1,250 in my savings and checking accounts, $4,200 in non-retirement investments and $5,000 in a Roth IRA. I earn $3,500 a month and have full health coverage with my employer. I owe $32,500 on my student loans plus the loan on my new pickup and am making $280 in payments each month to pay off these debts. I am also paying $50 a month to pay off the $750 balance on my credit card. My credit score is 650.

"I will keep building for my future without going crazy with purchases. In the next two years, I will have positioned myself for marriage. I will increase my income through a promotion or new job, will double the value of my Roth and non-Roth portfolios, have at least $5,000 in the bank, and have cut my loan debt to at least $20,000. I will also own a flat-screen television and a high-quality road bicycle. I may be taking night or online courses toward earning my master's degree.

"In five years, I will have no more student-loan or car debt, will have continued building up my Roth and non-retirement investments, and will have secured a house mortgage. I also will have traveled in Africa for at least three weeks. I may own and operate a small business by this time, such as being a consultant.

"In 10 years, I will be raising a family. I will have two children. I will retire by age 65, by which time I will have paid off my house and have bought homes in two different locations that will allow me to enjoy balmy weather year round and to golf regularly. I will live off the interest from my investments."

Once you've each written a financial goal statement, it's time to review each other's goal statements and then, create a *joint statement*. Assimilate the points of each other's goals into one statement reflecting what you want together. Here's an example of a joint statement:

Justin and Sarah's Joint Statement

"We are ages 27 and 24. Together we have $4,750 in our savings and checking accounts, $4,200 in investments other than retirement funds, and $16,600 in our retirement accounts. We're living in separate apartments on which we can afford the rent. We earn $7,300 a month and have full health coverage with our employers. We owe $68,200 on our student and car loans plus a medical debt, and are making $490 in payments each month to pay off these debts. We are paying $135 a month to retire the $1,950 balances on our credit cards. Our credit scores are 650 and 575.

"In the next two years, we will be married and sharing a rented apartment, condo, or house with at least three rooms. We will increase our incomes through promotions or new jobs and possibly a home-based business on the side. Justin will double his 401(k) savings, and Sarah will double the value of her non-retirement invest-ments. We will cut our loan debts in half and pay off our credit cards, and each of us will have credit scores of at least 700. We will own a flat-screen television, a high-quality road bicycle, a new sailboard, and a new hybrid or electric vehicle to replace Sarah's old Honda. Justin will have his master's degree. Sarah will be certified as a Pilates instructor.

> Often, couples meet with a priest, minister, or rabbi before marriage to discuss family issues. Why don't they meet with a financial consultant for a one-hour session to discuss financial issues?
>
> —Lee Slater, divorce financial analyst

"In five years, we will have no more student-loan or car debt, will have at least doubled our income invested for retirement, and will have secured a mortgage on a house within easy driving distance from Sarah's parents or sisters. We will have traveled in Africa for at least three weeks and windsurfed in the Caribbean for at least three weeks.

"In 10 years, we will have two healthy children. We will have them educated in private schools or progressive charter schools. Sarah will be working no more than part-time outside of the home until the youngest child is at least 6 years old. We will pay for their music, dance, or sports lessons—depending on their talents and interests—and pay for them to pursue undergraduate degrees at the colleges of their choice. Sarah may elect to have plastic surgery following the second childbirth.

"We will each retire by age 65, by which time we will have paid off our house and have bought homes in two different locations that will allow us to enjoy balmy weather year round and to golf, windsurf, or kayak regularly. We will live off the interest from our investments."

An Invaluable Step to Take

Review the information you've recorded in the table on page 16—what each of you owns and owes, and your incomes. It's advisable to take a little extra time beyond that to obtain your individual credit reports and review those together. Finally, review each of your financial goals. Make sure that each of you has a clear picture of who the other person is financially.

Financial planner Lee Slater offers an added step that engaged partners should take:

"Often, couples meet with a priest, minister, or rabbi before marriage to discuss family issues. Why don't they meet with a financial consultant for a one-hour session to discuss financial issues and pinpoint areas that need addressing? It would be extremely valuable to have these issues on the table, and hopefully resolved, before tying the knot."

Financial planners are listed in telephone directories and on the Internet. One way to verify if a planner is reputable is on the website of the Certified Financial Planner Board of Standards (www.cfp.net). Hourly rates generally range from $100 to $325.

Now that you've examined your respective money personalities, financial situations, and goals, each of you should have a much clearer picture about what sort of person you are considering marrying. The next chapter brings this picture into even sharper focus: guaranteeing that your partner is representing himself or herself honestly.

> "Oh what a tangled web we weave/
> When first we practice to deceive!"
> —Sir Walter Scott

3
Looking into Your Partner's Past

SOME MARRIAGE-MINDED folk conceal facts about their backgrounds. These include arrest records, previous marriages, and current marital status. Some unscrupulous sorts even assume fake identities.

Checking on Your Partner's Background

If you're going to take the major step of marrying someone, you need to know as much as possible about this person before walking down the aisle. Employers perform background checks before hiring employees. The stakes are infinitely higher in a marriage. "Why not legitimize the relationship by checking on your partner?" says licensed private detective Gordon Butler.

If you have significant financial assets, it's especially prudent to ensure the person you intend to marry has not misrepresented himself or herself just to get hold of your wealth. Over his four-decade career, Butler has conducted several hundred background checks for clients who wanted to know more about a potential mate. Usually the clients were wealthy, with assets to lose and questions about their love interest's personal history.

One client was a millionaire. His fiancée told him her parents were wealthy. She introduced him to them at a restaurant. He suspected she was not being truthful. He hired Butler to check out the parents. Sure enough, the fiancée had misled the client. He broke off the engagement.

"If you've got something to lose, then you need to do a background check," Butler says. Beyond money, people stand to "lose" by having a heart broken if they marry a dishonest person.

Common sense dictates that if a person you're considering marrying lies to you about his or her family, employment, financial situation, criminal record, marital history, or even name and age, that's grounds for terminating the relationship. "I wouldn't want them anywhere near me," Butler says of liars. "Normal people are not going to be phonies."

Again, the most likely targets for phonies are people with significant assets. Young couples just starting out in adult life usually have not amassed significant assets and also have fewer worries about each other's history than older people who have lived longer. But anyone getting married should feel comfortable about having a clear picture of who the other person is.

> Normal people are not going to be phonies.
> —Gordon Butler, private investigator

So where do you start in verifying key facts about your potential mate? And what level do you take it to? A good place to begin is with an open discussion. Here is a list of basic pieces of information you should seek from your partner before moving ahead toward marriage:

Legal name and age. If you've grown up with this person or have known the person for several years or more, you may not have many concerns or questions about the person's background. But if he or she is relatively new in your life, ask for an I.D. ("In a heartbeat, you want to see a driver's license," Butler says.)

Family. Again, if you've known this person for a good length of time, you may already know the person's background. But if you haven't done so already, you'll want to meet each other's parents (and other immediate relatives) to know what sort of family you're marrying into.

Employment. If you've been dating someone seriously, you've likely learned how he or she is employed, and you've possibly even visited the workplace. If you are in the dark about your partner's occupation, you should take the step of verifying where the person works. Maybe stop by and visit. Or call the place of employment and ask to speak to your partner.

Driving record. Moving violations affect car-insurance rates, as well as driving privileges. Unpaid tickets can mean an arrest warrant being issued. All this can affect your financial future. Ask your partner about his or her driving history.

Criminal record. You want to ensure your partner is of sound moral character. A criminal record that includes a felony can impair a person's ability to secure a good job. Ask your partner about any arrests or convictions. If confusion arises about the status of any incident, you can propose having your partner visit the local police station and ask the staff to run a criminal background check. There may be a fee charged. Ask your partner to bring you the printout. That way, the two of you can see what the actual rap sheet is.

Sexual history. Anyone engaging in sexual relations is advised to practice safer sex, which includes the person and his or her partner sharing their sexual histories and information about any sexually transmitted diseases they may have contracted. An STD can prove financially, as well as emotionally, costly.

Marital history. Anyone with a dating history accumulates not only experience but, perhaps, financial baggage. If either of you has been divorced or has offspring, you must share this information—including any financial obligations from those circumstances.

Credit report. The three national credit bureaus—Equifax, Experian, and TransUnion—maintain credit histories on individuals. A credit report contains the past seven years of a person's use of credit cards and bank loans, car loans and student loans, and other documented uses of credit. Credit reports list delinquent payments and their frequency, outstanding loans, number of credit applications, and any declaration of bankruptcy. Credit reports, therefore, provide a snapshot of a person's use of credit and the person's ability to repay loans. "It shows whether you're in a ton of debt before you get married, which can mean whether your spouse gets stuck with all the debt," Butler says.

The Fair Isaac Corporation uses these credit reports to calculate your FICO score—your credit score. Lenders such as banks rely heavily on credit scores to determine whether to give a loan and what interest rate to charge. A credit score is like a financial report card.

Your partner's financial habits and credit standing as well as your own will have a bearing on your marriage. So it's valuable for each of you to obtain your credit reports and review them together. Building a sound credit history can improve a credit score and one's chances of obtaining favorable mortgages and other loans. Reviewing credit reports can help the two of you strategize your financial futures together. It also may reveal a red flag—that your partner is too in debt or financially irresponsible to risk marrying. (What if your partner balks at reviewing his or her credit report with you? That's another red flag: refusing to be transparent.)

By federal law, you are entitled to a free credit report once a year from each of the three national credit bureaus. You can obtain the reports online at various websites. For an additional charge, you can order your credit score.

Tell your partner you'll be ordering your credit report and credit score and want him or her to do the same, so you can sit together and review them. (You can only order your own report, not someone else's.)

When to Do Detective Work

If something seems suspicious or unclear in your mind about any aspect of your partner's past or present and you want to do some digging around yourself, the Internet is a useful tool. A bit of additional legwork at government agencies can flesh out a background search.

See what entering your partner's name on Google or another search engine brings up. It's the same with surfing for information on your partner's family members. You can't gain access to someone else's credit report or health examinations by yourself, but you usually can obtain a driving record. Most jurisdictions charge a small fee for this record. Contact your local department of motor vehicles.

You can see if your partner's name comes up in cases on the courthouse websites of counties where you know he or she has lived. If feasible, visit the courthouse clerk's office in person and see what records exist on your partner regarding civil and criminal cases, and marriage and divorce records.

Another method is using an online people-search service. This can help you find certain information, including your partner's present and prior addresses, marriage and divorce records, criminal and civil court cases, and property and asset ownership. A nationwide search can cost about $35. Butler, however, considers these online services to be inadequate: "The only thing they can do is query public records, and they have a lot of old data."

Private investigators, in contrast, can dig up a world of accurate and useful information. You will need to provide the detective with the subject's full legal name and birth date. "If I get a Social Security number, I'm even better off," Butler says. Additional information that can be beneficial includes the subject's city of birth, current physical address, and jurisdictions where he or she has lived.

Hiring a detective is a surreptitious move. It's also a drastic one. Your partner could grow very upset knowing his or her background was being investigated, so you are cautioned to do this on the sly. The best way to find a reputable private investigator is via word of mouth. Butler suggests talking to a lawyer you respect and asking whom the lawyer would hire as a private eye. Expect to pay between $250 and $500 for a background check. Results should come within a week.

"You usually only hire a private investigator as a last resort, when you have some real doubt about whom you're talking to," Butler says.

"Debts and lies are generally mixed together."
—Francois Rabelais

4
Red Flags and Bad Scenarios

FOR TWO people seeing each other romantically, there's no escaping the subject of money. While it's considered tacky to discuss one's net worth early in the dating process (and it's rude to inquire), the matter of moolah appears practically from the start.

Who pays for the first date? How expensive is the first date? How does the way each person dresses and the car or other mode of transportation used measure up in the other's eyes? Finding out what the other does for a living is a subject that is certain to come up in conversation. It's the same with each other's living arrangements.

As time goes on and the relationship progresses, the two of you must come to terms with money issues, such as who covers the bill on a date, what sort of travel arrangements you'll have if you take trips together, how expensive are the gifts you give each other, and so on.

If you plan to marry—and stay married—you'll need to agree on fundamental financial issues that include the earning of income, setting a budget, allocating excess income, and investing for the future. If you're seeing a person and can't even agree on who foots the bill on a date or how expensive birthday or holiday gifts should be, this person may not be a partner with whom you can see eye to eye when it comes to the financial affairs of husband and wife.

Differences are normal and inevitable, says marriage and family therapist Kevin Roth, whose specialties include couples communication: "Compatibility means how we deal with our differences. With financial compatibility, if you have differences around how you spend money or what money means to each of you, it's really how you deal with those differences that is important."

Working through those differences includes not making the other person "wrong" for wanting to be different. One person may see sticking to a tight budget as very important; the other may say that's being too uptight. "In a two-person relationship there's your truth, my truth, and our truth," Roth says. "You want to create our truth—a win-win situation each of you can live with.

"If you can't work through those differences on your own, to me that's a red flag that you're going to need some help from a third party, such as a tax accountant, a financial advisor, or a family therapist."

Red Flags

Here are some red flags that can reveal serious challenges to achieving financial compatibility.

An inability to talk about money. "If the couple is not comfortable talking about money or if they try talking about money and the conversation goes nowhere or either partner continually changes the subject when the topic of money is discussed, that's a red flag," says marriage and family therapist Kristy Archuleta.

You might not see eye to eye on every issue regarding money, but you do need to be able to discuss money—even if it invites an argument. "I worry more about couples who don't fight at all than I worry about the ones who do, because completely ignoring something means they are not talking about it," Archuleta says.

"One of the partners may be suppressing feelings or desires to make the other one happy. This type of behavior can result in long-term damage, such as resentment toward the other person."

Never being able to see eye to eye on money. Coming to terms with each other on financial issues is a healthy sign. The ability to openly discuss each other's emotions indicates not only maturity, but also demonstrates a level of compatibility.

You should be able to come to a consensus on certain financial decisions in regard to your married life. The first point of agreement is that you will be making financial decisions jointly. You will be working closely together, including setting and maintaining a budget. The second point of agreement is that you will be creating a set of short-term and long-term goals. (An example of a short-term goal is setting aside cash in an emergency fund to cover at least three months income, as insurance against an unexpected loss of income or unforeseen expense. An example of a long-term goal is reaching certain investment objectives.)

Being deep in debt. One of the most important traits your partner should possess is how to manage money—at least in an elementary way. So, if your partner is utterly frivolous, irresponsible, and perhaps delusional about his or her own finances, that's a blazing red warning sign.

If your partner is deep in the financial hole, you must figure out how he or she got there—and what he or she plans to do to extricate himself/herself from this money trap. Have credit cards helped get him or her into this mess? Can your partner commit to cutting up all those cards or refrain from using them?

If this person is genuinely ready to correct past monetary mistakes, then his or her being in debt is not necessarily a deal killer. But you should consider keeping property legally separate to protect it from the indebted partner's creditors.

You or your partner has standing financial obligations that will carry on during the marriage. Does your partner owe alimony or child support from a previous marriage? Or is your partner raising children or paying for them to get through school? Perhaps your partner has a significant legal settlement to pay or medical expenses to pay off.

These are significant financial burdens that—while legally not your responsibility, perhaps even after marrying this partner—can weigh down financial progress for a couple. It also can fill you with resentment as you watch money that could be building your future going to support someone else's life. And if it's you bringing the financial baggage into the marriage, you must be prepared for resentment from your spouse when it comes to bill-paying time.

Court judgments such as child support or alimony may involve more than just the current monetary obligations. Additional court battles may be forthcoming on these issues as your partner or the ex-spouse may try to alter arrangements. This would cost you time, energy, and legal fees.

Your partner seems to have an inordinate amount of money or other assets. If your partner has an unexpectedly large bank account, it may indicate your partner is a tremendous saver, perhaps in a miserly fashion, and will be very reluctant to spend money after you're married. It also may mean your partner has lived with his or her parents longer than usual or necessary, mooching off them and avoiding the higher cost of living separately as an adult. That raises the issue of your partner's maturity level and ability to set up a household.

Possession of assets such as expensive cars or jewelry, or extra cash on hand that seems unusual for your partner's earning power could be a sign that your partner is involved in illegal activity.

Your money personalities don't work together. As discussed in Chapter 1, some money personalities seem well suited to each other, and some seem destined for tremendous failures or clashes. Still, traits are not absolute. A typical Puppy Dog isn't necessarily entirely irresponsible about spending, and a typical Squirrel is not necessarily completely rigid about saving. Two Puppy Dogs can learn to budget their income in a healthy way and pursue investment goals. And two Squirrels can stretch themselves to loosen the purse strings to enjoy the fruits of their savings.

Many people marry opposite money personalities and help balance each other, Archuleta says. Those who marry similar money personality types can, in the long run, develop opposite money personality types. For example, a saver (Squirrel) may marry a saver and eventually develop more of a spender (Puppy Dog) personality while the partner becomes even more of a saver.

"Money personalities change over time due to influences from family, friends, media, education, and personal experience," Archuleta says.

Common Scenarios That Lead to Strife

Since money conflicts are the biggest source of strife in a marriage, it's important to be aware of common scenarios that contribute to discord. And you must decide if each of you is mature enough to back up the other and not let the following scenarios prove volatile—and ultimately fatal—to the marriage.

You are doing well financially as a couple, but lack sufficient down time to spend with each other. One or each of you feels distant from the other. You are growing apart.

One partner is the breadwinner, and the other is the domestic engineer taking care of the home. The homemaker may feel trapped, inferior, unappreciated, and angry that the other partner doesn't pitch in to help with household duties. The income earner may feel unsupported and overburdened in bringing home the bacon. Each partner will feel resentful and misunderstood.

"Most women are in the workforce now, and most households require two incomes, yet women are still expected to be a breadwinner *and* do the housework," says lawyer Marilyn York, whose firm handles 150 to 200 divorce-related cases a year in California and Nevada.

One partner earns less than the other. The lower-earning partner feels subordinate and unworthy of giving input on money decisions. This lack of empowerment and self-esteem does not foster a healthy relationship and inevitably will breed con-flict. This scenario can become even more complicated if the woman earns more than the man. Cultural stereotypes hold that the husband should be the big breadwinner. If the wife earns

> If the couple is not comfortable talking about money, or if they try talking about money and the conversation goes nowhere, or either partner continually changes the subject when the topic of money is discussed, that's a red flag.
> — Kristy Archuleta, marriage and family therapist

more, the man can feel emasculated; the wife may feel self-conscious about being married to a man whom her family and friends regard as inadequate.

One spouse tends to spend money without consulting the other. The spender may be buying something for his or her business or job, yet the expenditure impacts the household budget. Or the spender may just be copying how his or her own parents bought things. Or the spender may be a compulsive buyer and seek to hide this behavior. The spender often doesn't understand that it makes the other partner feel frustrated, unimportant, devalued, and disrespected.

Both of you are spenders who can't seem to rein in your deficit spending. Neither is able or willing to budget like an adult. Creditors are calling and calling. Or the car breaks down, and there isn't any credit left to cover repairs.

"This is a couple that's always in a state of panic," York says. "Imagine how it impacts marital bliss."

Both of you are savers, and inevitably unhappiness builds in the marriage from an inability to loosen up and enjoy life. This is a case of money ironically standing in the way of a couple's success, says York: "If you're not willing to buy a nicer house or bigger house and won't go on dates because you don't want to eat out or spend money on entertainment, and you won't go on vacations, you'll get stuck in a rut. And you'll potentially be at each other's throats. Or die bored.”

One of you has to work two jobs to support the household. This wears down the two-job holder. Ironically, the other partner resents not having enough time to spend with the first partner. Even worse is if both of you work two jobs to support the household.

“Sometimes you have to reevaluate your financial compatibility. You have to evolve,” York says. “For example, kids have a huge financial impact on a marriage. This should be discussed in advance of getting pregnant—how much it’s going to cost and how you’ll meet these additional financial and familial responsibilities.”

One of you works outside the home a great deal. Trouble starts if that person is not physically and/or emotionally present for the family.

Beware the Midlife Crisis

A marital partner may seem happy and content, but—seemingly out of the blue—experience an internal crisis that calls for a drastic change. According to family therapist Kevin Roth, when individuals hit certain age milestones, such as 30 or 40, they are prone to examine their lives and rethink the rules by which they’ve been playing. If they are feeling dissatisfaction or remorse, they may very well blame their partners.

So it’s important to understand that a relationship that seems to be cruising smoothly along can hit a rocky road caused by internal, not external, factors.

One Couple’s Story

Before Sue met Gary, she seriously dated a Puppy Dog and an Ostrich and was briefly married to a Sparrow. None of these relationships worked out for Sue, a lifelong Squirrel.

When she left home at 17 to join the counterculture scene in Hollywood in 1969, she brought a $20 bill. She never spent it, preferring to panhandle, sell newspapers, and sleep in crash pads.

When Sue met Gary, she was a divorcée in her early 30’s with an 18-month-old daughter. He was in his late 20’s, an equipment designer in the music industry who played in bands for fun. He was several thousand dollars in debt and owned just what his rented apartment held. He was a Puppy Dog—but after meeting Sue, he quit his partying ways and resolved to become financially solvent.

Sue had just purchased a condominium and knew it'd be tough meeting the mortgage. But two incomes could manage that. What's more, Gary was the perfect father to Sue's daughter. They married.

Nearly 25 years later, their marriage has been a success. They've raised their daughter (whom Gary adopted) and a son they had together. They've worked out their money-management system. Sue the Squirrel is in charge. A bookkeeper by profession, she handles the bills and investing.

"I manage every penny, and I like to put stuff away," she says. "I tend to over budget. I'm kind of a control freak. I'm always afraid of not having any money. It's to the point where his paycheck goes into the bank through direct deposit; he doesn't touch it.

"If he wants money, he comes to me. He has access to the account through credit cards. He can be impulsive sometimes. If he wants something—music or computer equipment or something for his bicycle—he'll put it on a credit card. He usually lets me know before the fact. There've been a couple of surprises, but there weren't big-dollar surprises."

Money hasn't proved an absolute ruler of their lives. Gary was CEO of a company in Marin County, Calif., earning a good income. But in 2001 he and Sue decided to relocate to Reno, Nev., for a lower-key lifestyle and to be closer to skiing at Lake Tahoe.

Sue maintains their frugal lifestyle. "We do own our house and are able to make our mortgage payment every month and pay a little extra to knock down the principal. I have never had a car loan or anything that I haven't paid off early."

Gary's work hours dropped during the recession, and Sue was laid off from her job. "We've cut out all extras, including eating out and spending money on going out to bars and shows. We do a lot of stuff for fun, but without paying. For recreation, we ride bikes. During ski season, we had a season's pass. I work at a local community theater, and we get to see shows for free. We go to free music gigs. I don't pay for pricy drinks; once in a while, I'll order a club soda."

As a scrupulous Squirrel, Sue set up a separate bank account that Gary is aware of, but knows is off limits for withdrawals—or even discussion. Sue has put six months of income into this account as an emergency fund. She is restarting her own business as a bookkeeper and QuickBooks software advisor.

"Just recently, we've started having money conversations about what are our retirement goals and how we're going to get there," Sue says. "We've invested in retirement funds; we haven't touched that money because we can't without a penalty. We're looking at maybe investing in a house because it's a good time to buy."

> "Coming together is a beginning; keeping together is progress; working together is success."
> — Henry Ford

5

Living Together versus Marrying?

ONE APPROACH to determining compatibility is to take a trial run. Meaning: Live together before marriage. An estimated 4 million couples in America are living out of wedlock. (That contrasts to about 52 million couples who are married.)

Marriage brings with it a slate of financial and legal responsibilities. Partners might not be entirely certain about each other or even themselves and crave more time to get to know each other before taking the plunge. Another motive for living together before marriage is to allow each partner to stabilize personal finances. The saying, "Two can live as cheaply as one" has real merit, considering the cost of housing.

A Note of Caution about Cohabitation

Research suggests that living together before marriage *does not* better the odds of staying together permanently after the knot is legally tied. A study funded by the National Institute of Child Health and Human Development reported that in the United States, couples who live together are at a greater risk for divorce. Couples who cohabitate before marriage are between 1.26 and 1.86 times more likely to divorce. But research also found that if cohabitation is limited to a person's future spouse, the risk of divorce is not heightened. Cohabitating couples who take premarital education courses or counseling are at no greater risk for divorce.

Marriage, simply by its emotional and legal status, can drastically alter the dynamics of a relationship of two partners who had been living together. "What changes are those introjects—those tapes running through your mind about what a marriage should be like," says marriage and family therapist Kevin Roth. "It all changes when the rice hits the floor."

When a couple cohabitates, they have the option of easily and freely leaving the relationship. "Once the marriage is official, couples often have a hard time adjusting to the new commitment," says therapist Kristy Archuleta. "The phrase that marriage is just a piece of paper usually doesn't square with reality."

When partners live together, it's more of a roommate-like, voluntary relationship. As soon as people marry—and it's an involuntary relationship—they become less forgiving of faults and more expectant of the partner living up to certain ideals, says divorce lawyer Marilyn York. These may be ideals that people don't even know they keep in their heads and hark back to previous generations.

> Once the marriage is official, couples often have a hard time adjusting to the new commitment. The phrase that marriage is just a piece of paper usually doesn't square with reality.
> —Kristy Archuleta, marriage and family therapist

"A man can fix on an image of his mother and her role in the household, while the woman has images of her dad, and each image fosters antiquated expectations," York says. "The man may blurt out, 'How come you're not doing the dishes? You're the wife.' Or the woman may say, 'The yard work's your work. You go mow the lawn.' But when they were living together before marriage, he didn't mind cleaning the sink, and she was happy to cut the grass."

Monetary, Tax, and Credit Implications

There are a number of potential complications for couples who live together without getting married.

- If one partner dies, the other won't automatically inherit a portion of the other's assets.
- If the partners split, even if they've lived together a long time, neither will automatically get to keep a certain amount of assets that would be due to partners who were married.

- The poorer partner won't be able to claim alimony to live on.
- If one partner declares bankruptcy, he or she won't be able to take advantage of laws that allow a married partner to own property in joint names, exempt from creditors' claims.
- An unmarried couple may not be able to adopt.
- If the couple has a child out of wedlock, the father is liable for child support, but may have to take extra steps to guarantee his visitation rights to the child should the couple split. (The father is advised to sign the birth certificate and also have a legal document drafted by a lawyer and notarized stating that the man is the father.)
- If one partner has been transferred for work, the other may not be able to claim unemployment benefits in some states.

Couples who opt to live together outside of marriage should take certain precautions to avoid financial complications. Each partner should have a will, and assets should be kept in separate accounts.

Married couples can also face potential complications.

- In two special cases in which a person's spouse has died, marriage may have financial drawbacks for the survivor. If a person is younger than 60 and remarries, he or she could lose Social Security benefits based on the deceased spouse's work record. Military plans also may suspend pension-survivor benefits if the surviving spouse marries before age 55.
- A two-income married couple usually pays more in income taxes than the collective taxes of an unmarried couple. Accountants call this the marriage penalty. In a single-income household, however, a married couple enjoys a second personal-exemption deduction.

Common-law Marriages

Ten states and the District of Columbia recognize common-law marriages in which the states treat a couple as married if the couple holds itself to the community as married. These states are Alabama, Colorado, Kansas, Rhode Island, South Carolina, Iowa, Montana, Oklahoma, Texas, and Utah. Four states have "grandfathered" common-law marriage (Georgia, Idaho, Ohio, and Pennsylvania).

If you establish a common-law marriage in one of these states and move to a state without common-law marriages, that state may consider you officially married anyway. You'll have to check that state's laws to be sure.

One Couple's Story

Although living together before marriage often fails to translate into long-term relationship survival for the majority of couples, it worked out for Gayle and John, who shared a house for a half-year before tying the knot.

Certain factors and circumstances were in motion that perhaps guaranteed the couple's success. When the two met on a blind date, they discovered to their mutual surprise that they matched up extremely well. Each had dated enough and was only interested in finding a partner for life. Each was tall. Each worked in the media industry. And when Gayle visited John's apartment, she was stunned to find he had teak furniture as did she.

Time played a role, too. The three people renting rooms from Gayle happened to be moving out. John lived in a suburb 30 miles from Gayle's house, a miserable commute in Seattle's congested freeway traffic. When John moved in with Gayle in April, three months after they first met, "really it was about timing and economic issues," Gayle says. "It was ridiculous for us to travel back and forth all the time. We had already picked out our wedding date and knew we would be officially engaged soon. We were awaiting a family ring."

The ring would include a diamond from a pinky ring that John's mother owned. His parents already had flown out from the East Coast to meet Gayle. John had met Gayle's parents. He and Gayle opened a joint checking account. The little voice in Gayle's head questioning if they were rushing things never grew too shrill. Love had the last word in her internal debate.

As for John, he knew their cohabitation was no trial run. "It was basically the start of our run," he says. "We had already promised our loyalty and love to each other. We may not have been married in a lawful way, but we were promised to each other and knew we would stick with it."

Everything fell into place in quick fashion, and that October the couple was married on a date that fit with John's work schedule and allowed a honeymoon. Fourteen years later, they are still married. Now in their mid-40's, they have two children and have worked hard on communication skills.

The two offer several reasons why living together before tying the knot didn't negatively impact their subsequent marriage:

They shared similar values, and each wanted children. They even had similar decorating tastes.

Each was financially independent and progressing in a career. (John produced a local television show covering a sports team. Gayle was a business manager for a radio station group.)

Each was tired of dating games and was old enough to be serious about commitment. Gayle was 32, John was 30.

They communicated clearly and thoroughly with each other. "We spent a lot of time talking about lifestyle and children, those fundamentals," Gayle says. "It wasn't all candles and romance."

> "Money, if it does not bring you happiness, will at least help you be miserable in comfort."
> —Helen Gurley Brown

6
Genders Differ on Financial Needs

IT'S ALWAYS dangerous, from a standpoint of accuracy, to use generalizations in describing behaviors specific to either gender. But some mental-health counselors and financial experts note certain patterns for men and women in our culture when it comes to money.

Recognizing these patterns can help a couple prepare for the gender dynamics that could come into play in their financial life.

Gender Differences and Money

Men dislike discussing investment choices with their mates, while women are compelled to discuss financial issues with their spouses. In general, women feel the need to talk over financial decisions more than men do.

"Men tend to communicate to give a command or an order," says Kevin Roth. "Women tend to communicate to join and connect. So if they're discussing finances, the man might grow irritable at the woman's questions, taking it to mean that she's second-guessing or criticizing his judgment. Therefore, he may grow defensive. But to her, communication means something different. She wants to share her feelings and his. She just wants to talk about the finances."

Women also prefer more time to analyze and determine a course of action, whereas men are prone to make decisions quicker and move to action. Men also take more investment risks, while women are more conservative. Women are prone to lose less money and less often than men, but also miss out on the long-term investments that would yield bigger returns.

Men blame their women for financial woes, while women blame themselves, but can resent their men. Men take the glory for themselves when they make money, but fault others if they lose it. Women give credit to others when making money, but fault themselves when they lose it.

Men because of societal influences believe they should be the breadwinner in a marriage. Women because of societal influences believe the man should be the breadwinner—or at least women feel they should be able to explain why the man is not the breadwinner.

Women who feel financially dependent in a marriage are prone to be less vocal on financial matters—worrying that they won't be able to support themselves if the marriage ends. Men who experience a sense of failure as a breadwinner tend to withdraw into themselves, instead of communicating with their partner. They can compensate for their inferiority complex through an addiction of some kind—alcoholism, workaholism, or immersion in golf, fantasy baseball, poker, pornography, or some other diversion.

Women who lose faith in their men as breadwinners and are frustrated by the man's clamming up can give up and walk out on the relationship. This is especially true during a difficult financial time.

In general, men don't like to discuss their troubles. Women are the opposite—they share their emotions.

Equal Voices Equal Smart Decisions

No life is free from financial volatility. The economy itself is ever shifting cyclically from one phase to the next, whether expansion or contraction, prosperity or recession, bull market or bear market, boom or bust. Money woes of some degree can and will strike each couple.

The key to survival and forging ahead financially as well as matrimonially is sticking together instead of tearing each other apart. The blame game is costly—financially and emotionally. And it often leads to divorce.

The best marital atmosphere when it comes to finances is one in which each partner enjoys an equal say. If the relationship is lopsided, then the short-changed partner is bound to feel inferior and resentful. What's more, if one of the partners is prevented from developing money-management skills, this can prove disastrous over the long run. This partner may run up credit-card balances or insist on foolish moves—such as buying an overly expensive house—that will sabotage the couple's financial affairs, which in turn can precipitate divorce.

On the other hand, if the partners work together, sharing in money decisions, feeling an equal responsibility in financial affairs, and doing so in a spirit that is collegial instead of adversarial, then discussions and decisions about finances will be productive and less prone to involve fighting or (more insidiously) repressed anger that inevitably will explode when it can't be held in any longer.

It all boils down to this: Your partner must be willing and able to share fully in financial decisions with you, and vice-versa.

When it comes to a couple addressing the vital issue of how they will make their marriage financially viable, the most important qualities are communication and lack of fear, says financial advisor Mackenzie Waggaman, a vice president with American Investment Services, a financial-investment management service that is a wholly owned subsidiary of the American Institute for Economic Research.

> A lot of people are very fearful to talk about money. It's been ingrained in them that somehow it's not polite or it taints the blush of the relationship. But if you really love somebody, you want them cared for financially. A discussion about money should be a reinforcing of one's love commitment.
> —Mackenzie Waggaman, financial advisor

"A lot of people are very fearful to talk about money," Waggaman says. "It's been ingrained in them that somehow it's not polite to talk about money or it somehow taints the blush of the relationship. But if you really love somebody, you want them cared for financially. A discussion about money should be a reinforcing of one's love commitment. If you don't make smart decisions together, you're hurting each other. The first stress to the marriage is usually financial. If you don't work together on finances, you could be killing the marriage."

Waggaman's clients include long-married couples. "My most successful clients are couples who are both on the same page when it comes to their finances," he says. Waggaman has repeatedly seen the dreadful outcome when one of the spouses has made all the investment decisions and the other spouse has remained uninvolved and never developed financial knowhow. If the decision maker dies first, the surviving spouse not only feels confused about managing the portfolio—he or she is a target for predators pitching questionable investments for which they can charge exorbitant fees.

"Typically it's the husband who has never informed his wife about what's going on financially and has the opinion, whether factual or not, that she is not interested," Waggaman says. "After he dies, she's frightened about how to manage the finances and what to do with the assets. Some insurance agents and stockbrokers read the death notices; they will bombard her with calls. Before this poor woman even knows it, she's signed on the bottom line for annuity products or other investments. Opportunists will just take uninitiated widows or widowers to the cleaners.

"If only people understood what happens if there is inequality in knowledge of financing in a relationship. It's just tragic."

Marriage Cues Tapes Playing in Your Head

"When you get married, a lot of tapes play in your head about what a relationship should look like," says Kevin Roth. "It might not be a problem while you're dating, but all of a sudden, once you get married, these tapes start running."

The sources of these images—known as introjects—usually come from our childhood. We may expect that our marriage should mirror our parents'. For example, one of Roth's colleagues got married. The first day she and her husband were settled in after their honeymoon, he came home from work. Standing at the top of the stairs, she said, "Hi, honey." He said hi, walked into the kitchen, and made himself a sandwich. She was offended. Why? Because when she was a child, her father would come home from work, run upstairs and kiss her mother. Roth's colleague didn't understand why she was hurt until she analyzed the source of her feelings.

Newly married partners also harbor expectations for their financial relationship, although they're perhaps unconscious of the sources of those expectations. These expectations may be to replicate the relationship of their parents—such as the husband being the breadwinner, the wife managing the bills, or the family being scrupulous savers who live a thrifty life. Or perhaps one or each of the partners carries around resentment from childhood and wants a different lifestyle than what he or she had as a child. One partner's family may have constantly been in debt and perhaps lost their home. This partner craves security and wants to be financially conservative. Or a partner was frustrated in childhood by not being allowed to purchase the clothes, bicycle, or car. He or she never wants to live a tightwad existence again.

"Usually our frame of reference is where we grew up and what that means," Roth says. "If spending money was thought of as irresponsible, we may have a judgment about that. Or, if we grew up without much money, we may want to live differently now."

> "Money is not the most important thing in the world.
> Love is. Fortunately, I love money."
> — Jackie Mason

7

Prenuptial and Postnuptial Agreements

IT HARDLY seems romantic for an engaged couple to hammer out legal documents specifying who owns what before a marriage and who will continue to own what during and (hypothetically) after a marriage. But if two people are mature enough to get married, they must be mature enough to see the world we live in. Life is not a fairy tale. Not every couple in love goes on to live happily ever after. The unexpected can occur. People change; circumstances change. No one can predict the future infallibly.

At a time in our society when the divorce rate hovers around 50 percent, a partner with substantial personal assets or business interests, or whose financial situation is much different from his or her partner's, is well advised to protect the property he or she brings into a marriage. A great many people do, which is why the term "prenup"—short for prenuptial—has entered everyday speech. Other terms used are premarital agreement or antenuptial agreement.

Prenups and the Law

The laws governing divorce already protect the interests of each partner to some degree. All U.S. states generally require an even split of all property acquired by both marital partners as a result of efforts spent during the marriage. In addition, courts in each state commonly award to spouses the rights to inherit a certain amount of property (a minimum of one-third, in most states). But a prenup gives partners greater control over their circumstances instead of leaving decisions in the hands of a court of law, which burns up time, energy, and legal fees. Some legal experts recommend that the richer spouse offer a gift at least equal to the share mandated by the state. (For example, one-third of the estate.) This transfer of assets will take place after a couple marries to avoid the gift tax.

Prenups actually have been in America for more than 100 years, beginning about the turn of the 20th century. They gained in common usage during the Roaring Twenties as prosperous men wed younger beauties and worried that these trophy wives would claim the men's fortunes through divorce or death. Courts, however, often did not enforce these prenup agreements, holding that such pacts ran counter to the spirit of public policy. But societal mores had changed drastically by the 1970's, and today most judges accept the terms of prenups as long as they meet certain legal requirements. Judges sometimes enforce portions of prenups while rejecting others.

> A prenup reveals your partner's true colors by showing how generous he or she will be toward you in a divorce scenario. And that's valuable, because you can rest assured that you'll see an uglier, less generous person if the two of you end up in the divorce process.
> —Marilyn York, divorce lawyer

Laws regarding divorce and prenups vary by state, but at present, 26 states have adopted some version of the Uniform Premarital Agreement Act, which sets standards for prenup contracts. Other states have written their own statutes regarding prenups, or use their own common law.

Some experts on marriage and divorce believe that prenups are usually a bad idea that bode ill for a marriage's success and cause unfair settlements. But other experts hold that prenups have a great many benefits—and not only to protect the legitimate interests of one or the other party. A prenup entered into openly and intelligently by two level-headed partners can help them clearly establish the ownership and management of assets during the marriage, thus helping them avoid these sources of conflict that bedevil a great many unions.

Finally, a prenup can save each partner legal expenses that would be expended—if the marriage ends—while pursuing a divorce settlement. However, a prenup is not an invincible legal document warding off any chance of a claim. And in an acrimonious divorce, a prenup actually can precipitate litigation.

"I've almost never seen a prenup *not* be challenged," says veteran divorce lawyer Marilyn York. "Almost always, they're upheld. But because they're contested, it means more legal fees."

Still, York sees more positive than negative aspects to a prenup. "It forces you to really learn about your spouse," she says. "You have to discuss finances and fully disclose your assets. What's more, it requires you to discuss a divorce scenario. Because of that, you can find out whether the person you're marrying—this person with whom you're lovey-dovey in the honeymoon phase of courtship—is actually a selfish jerk. A prenup reveals your partner's true colors by showing how generous he or she will be toward you in a divorce scenario. And that's valuable because you can rest assured that you'll see an uglier, less generous person if the two of you end up in the divorce process."

A prenup addresses sensitive issues that many partners don't consider before tying the knot. If the woman gets pregnant, for example, will she quit her job and stay home for a number of years to raise the child? If so, and the marriage dies, what will be her compensation for lost time in the labor force?

The process of creating a prenup can serve like an acid test defining a relationship's true strength. "With about a third of the prenups I've done, the discussion makes the wedding get called off," York says. "Some couples stay together without getting married. But they're in the minority. Nearly all couples who call off the wedding actually break up. The prenup brings to light issues that get one partner upset at the other."

Conditions That Suggest Creating a Prenup

A wide gap exists between the partners' individual wealth. The term "gold digger" is not pleasant, but was coined because some people do marry for money. A prenup can eliminate this motive so that the much wealthier partner knows that his or her betrothed is seeking to wed for love, not lucre.

Conversely, a much poorer partner can benefit from an equitable prenup that financially provides for him or her in the event of a divorce, so that the wealthier partner won't be able to use a stronger financial position as a weapon of control in the marriage should the relationship sour.

A wide gap exists between the partners' incomes. In many states, a prenup can limit the sum of alimony. (However, state child-support laws are unaffected by prenup agreements.)

A partner has significant debt. If the marriage ends, the other partner won't want to be obligated to pay for his or her partner's premarital debts. A prenup can specify this.

A partner owns a business. A divorce, with the divvying up of assets, can yield a partner a share of the other's business or businesses. This may especially be unwanted by the business partners. A prenup can prevent this. (A business's bylaws also can prevent this.)

A partner has important considerations in an estate plan. A prenup can prevent the other partner from overturning this plan, which may specify heirs and heirlooms. Since a prenup is signed by both parties, it can be easier for a court to uphold than a will.

A partner plans to become a stay-at-home parent. Quitting outside employment will impact this partner's income (and, potentially, future employment prospects). A prenup can ensure that the financial load of raising the children is borne fairly by each partner.

A partner is remarrying. Obligations from the first marriage, possibly including children from that union, may exist. The partner may also have significant assets, such as a house, from the previous marriage. A prenup can safeguard the distribution of assets according to the partner's wishes if he or she dies.

Family members are insistent on a prenup. Relatives, especially parents of younger people getting married, sometimes meddle. A prenup can quell their criticisms.

Basic Points to Know about Prenups

Know your state's laws. As mentioned earlier, laws governing marital property vary from state to state; they also are subject to change. Partners preparing a prenup agreement need to hire lawyers well versed in the laws. Make sure the agreement adheres to the Uniform Premarital Agreement Act, which has certain requirements and protections that makes a prenup consistent with laws in all 50 states. For example, the prenup must be in writing, and can only be revoked in writing.

Child support falls outside the purview of prenups. State laws governing child support supersede prenup terms.

Use independent counsels. Each partner should have his or her own lawyer review the prenup, in line with legal ethics that say no attorney should represent more than one interest in the same action. Terms of a prenup can be challenged on many grounds, including that one partner had inadequate legal representation when the document was created and signed.

A prenup must not be signed under pressure. Other grounds for challenging a prenup include whether the person creating the prenup used duress to force the other person to sign it. A judge could suspect this sort of unfair pressure is if the contract was signed a very short time before the wedding. A judge will seek to determine if undue influence was involved in coercing one party to sign the prenup. For example, suspicion would be aroused if one of the parties to the prenup was in a state of distress at the time the contract was signed. Yet another example of undue influence is if one partner is much older, much better educated, or has greater life experience. Yet another scenario that could prevent a judge from upholding a prenup is if its terms call for a gross inequality in the distribution of assets following a divorce. If one partner is much wealthier than the other, the judge is likely to scrutinize the settlement if its terms are one-sided.

Finances must be fully disclosed. A judge is especially prone to closely analyze whether each party to a prenup provided a full disclosure of his or her assets and debts. If a full disclosure did not occur, the agreement could be held to be invalid and unenforceable by the court. Items that require disclosure include income, anticipated future income, assets (including real estate and jewelry), inheritance and heirlooms, pensions and retirement plans, life insurance and beneficiaries, location of all accounts at financial institutions (such as banks and brokerages) and people at those institutions who handle those accounts, and alimony.

Create net-worth statements. To ensure a prenup's validity and decrease the chance it will be successfully challenged in court, net-worth statements for each partner should be executed before the marriage to document which property will remain separate and which will become joint after the marriage. (Definitions for separate property and joint property are given below.)

In sum: The terms of a prenup should be fair. It should be signed by two partners who clearly understand its terms, who have employed separate legal representation to review the terms, who are willing to abide by the terms, and who have fully disclosed their respective financial assets and debts before signing the document.

Basic Terminology Regarding Prenups

Equitable distribution. This is the scheme used in 41 states to divide assets upon divorce. These states use a common-law system. In equitable distribution, all property and debt is to be divided fairly upon divorce. In a lengthy marriage, the chance of an even split of assets is much greater than in a short marriage.

Community property. Community property is recognized in the nine states that have community-property laws. The term refers to all earnings and property acquired from those earnings during the course of a marriage, no matter who made the earnings. Similarly, all debts (such as mortgages, car loans, and credit-card transactions), taken on by either spouse and incurred during a marriage are considered community-property debt. Community property and debt are shared equally by the partners.

Current to publication of this book, community-property states are Arizona, California, Idaho, Louisiana, Nevada, New Mexico, Texas, Washington, and Wisconsin. Alaska allows married couples to create a written contract specifying that some or all of their property will be treated as community property. The U.S. territory of Puerto Rico also recognizes community property.

Separate property. This term—applicable in community-property states— refers to property owned and controlled solely by one spouse during a marriage. This property cannot be divided under property-division laws by the partners at divorce. Separate property includes that which a spouse acquired before the marriage, through inheritance or as a gift during the marriage, or after the date of separation of the marriage. It also includes any property generated from separate property (such as money from selling an inherited item).

Finally, separate property includes that which the partners legally agreed is separate. Similarly, separate debt is that which belongs to one spouse and includes debts incurred before the marriage or after the date of separation. (Accounts, such as for credit cards, owned jointly must be legally separated for a spouse to enjoy protection from debt incurred by the other on those accounts after the date of separation.) Of special note is that, in most states, neither spouse can be excluded from the other's dwelling, even if that dwelling is designated as separate property.

Date of separation. In general, this is the date marking the end of property being characterized as community property. What exactly marks the date from a legal standpoint is a gray area that can be open to the subjective interpretation of the court. Some states regard this date as when each spouse decides to end the marriage. Other states consider this the date when one of the spouses moved out of the marital home.

Marital asset. This term simply applies to all property acquired by either or both spouses during the course of a marriage, no matter who owns the property.

Joint property. This term means property with more than one owner. Community property is one of the basic forms of joint property. Another is joint tenancy, which in turn has different forms. This is important when it comes to probate law, which governs how ownership of the property (estate) that a person owned at the time of death is transferred to other parties (beneficiaries). In joint tenancy with right of survivorship, if one of the joint tenants dies, the surviving owner (or owners) will continue to own the asset, while any beneficiaries of the deceased will receive nothing. One form of joint tenancy of property in a marriage, recognized by some states, is called tenancy by entirety, and means that if one spouse dies, the survivor will own the property, and no other heirs will gain title to it. This avoids probate. Another form of joint tenancy is tenancy in common, and means that property is owned by two or more people, and each owner can sell his or her share of the property without consent of any other owner. This tenant can leave his or her interest in the property to a beneficiary. The property interest is subject to probate.

Estate plan. This refers to a plan that includes legal documents usually containing all or some of the following: the couple's will, living will, trusts (such as charitable remainder trusts, qualified personal-residence trusts, and life-insurance trusts), beneficiary designations, powers of appointment, powers of attorney (durable medical and durable financial), and property ownership (for example, joint tenancy with right of survivorship). In community-property states, the death of a spouse can mean that the intestacy laws of the state will determine where the property will go. (Intestacy refers to the condition of all or part of an estate of which the value exceeds enforceable debts and expense, yet has no beneficiaries specified by a valid will or other binding declaration.) However, if the couple had prepared an estate plan, it would supersede the state's laws.

Broaching the Subject of a Prenup

It may be tempting for a partner selling the mate-to-be on the idea of signing a prenup to claim the subject is being raised because his or her family demands it. Another excuse is blaming the need for a prenup on pressure from the partner's lawyer. But in the end, the partner is the one making the decision.

If a couple is ready for marriage, their relationship should be strong enough to withstand underlying tensions that could be brought to the surface by one partner raising the subject of a prenup. The positive aspects of the prenup should be emphasized: It will clarify financial issues so that they won't become sources of confusion or worry later on; it will serve the interests of close communication and foster better understanding of each other.

The sooner a couple discusses a prenup, the better. Avoiding the subject until the wedding day is near will likely increase the degree of anxiety and perhaps mistrust and anger of the partner being asked to sign. Once a prenup is arranged that is acceptable to each partner, they can enjoy a sense of relief. However, prenups should be periodically updated, divorce lawyer Marilyn York says:

"People don't always follow the specificity in a prenup. For example, they may end up comingling property that a prenup called separate. Prenups are only good for four or five years with the specificity in them. In a perfect legal world, people will look at their prenups every five years and see if they need to be updated. But this will bring up emotional issues each time and could tip people toward divorce, given all the other issues that surface in a marriage over time."

Postnups

Postnuptial agreements serve purposes similar to a prenuptial agreement. The main difference is that postnups are created during a marriage instead of before. Sometimes, postnups are written to clarify financial arrangements between the partners, including serious issues that may have emerged; other times, postnups are used to update prenups. To withstand any possible court challenges, postnups require the same full disclosures as prenups and separate counsel for each partner.

Key differences between prenups and postnups arise from the fact that prenups are agreements between two partners who aren't married yet, while postnups are contracts between partners who are already married and whose life circumstances have changed because of that marriage. Courts have tended to overturn postnups more often than prenups; the reason very well may be that judges are concerned that one spouse may have become greatly dependent on the other and therefore has a much weaker (and therefore unfair) negotiating position in hammering out the terms of the postnup.

One Couple's Story

When Roberta met Randy, he hardly seemed a catch. She was 19, and he was 35 and going through a nasty and financially ruinous divorce. She worked for the struggling company, a manufacturer of paint applicators, that Randy and his brother owned, and which was losing money.

When Roberta started dating Randy, she gave up her job to avoid the ramifications of being romantically involved with an employer and moved in. After Randy popped the marriage question, Roberta offered to sign a prenuptial agreement. She'd seen how Randy's ex-wife had gobbled up nearly all of the property from their marriage. Nearly two-thirds of his income was going to pay alimony plus child support for his two children with his ex.

"His ex-wife was taking everything she could get her hands on," Roberta says. "I wanted him to know I wasn't like that. I wasn't marrying him for money or anything other than that I loved him."

But Randy declined the prenup. "It would forever have cast a shadow on my feelings and commitment to her," he says. "A prenup to me was a sign of mistrust. Both of us felt we needed to be together, and I didn't want to start off with the first note being a hesitation. A prenup was never a serious consideration for me."

Roberta's offering of the prenup, though, confirmed to Randy how much she cared for him. And Randy's deciding against the prenup underscored for Roberta his trust in her.

The couple pulled together and weathered economic duress. They had two children in the first four years of marriage. Roberta was a full-time homemaker, while Randy toiled endless hours at the company. "I was more married to the business than my family," he says. "We lived hand to mouth for two to three years, before the business began taking off. Five years later, we were well off. We saw the extremes."

Randy and his brother built up their company to 135 employees and made it so profitable that when they sold it in 2000, each partner realized several million dollars. Randy retired and now spends his time renovating homes, managing his family's investments, and enjoying life with his wife and their three children.

As he and Roberta realized hard-won wealth, there was never a need for a postnupial agreement. They consider each other equal partners in their good fortune. "Having her and the relationship inspired me to do even better in business and apply myself even more to provide for our future," Randy says after 18 years of marriage. "We both feel like we equally shared in getting ourselves to where we are in our lives today."

The one legal consideration he attended to that is contained in some prenups is that, when he and his brother still owned their business, they had their company's bylaws state that if either partner died, his widow would be paid off for one-half the value of the business, but have no control of the business. Each brother also took out a life-insurance policy with the same specification.

"There's probably a lot of valid reasons for a prenup," Randy says. "But I'm an optimist, and generally a pessimist is going to be more inclined to want a prenup—or a person who is very greedy. Greed is a big motivator for those things. It's saying, 'I'm preparing myself that this might not work out.'

"Every couple goes through their fair share of trials. Roberta and I are no different. But when you get to a tough point in your life together, you both need to look at the other person and say, 'I'm totally committed to you and whatever we're going through.' At that point, you're really a team. You're not the person who's thinking, 'Yeah, we're married, but I know where the backdoor is.'

"In my situation, I weighed everything with Roberta and thought a prenup would do more damage potentially in feelings and trust than good. It wasn't a good fit for us."

Says Roberta: "Our marriage is really good, and it's forever. Divorce is not an option in our minds. Whatever we go through, we work through. I didn't marry him for his money, so the prenup was just silly for us."

"I dreamed of a wedding of elaborate elegance/A church filled with family and friends/I asked him what kind of a wedding he wished for/He said one that would make me his wife."

— Anonymous

8

Wedding Bell Tolls

IN THE olden days, a father provided a dowry along with his daughter's hand in marriage. In more recent times, custom called for the bride's family to foot the bill for the wedding while the groom or his family covered the bachelor party, honeymoon, and home.

Times continue to change, and many families in America regard the steep cost of weddings as an unfair burden for one side to bear alone. In 2009, about 40 percent of couples were paying for the ceremony and reception themselves, and about 60 percent had at least some contributions from their families, according to Samantha Goldberg, a veteran wedding planner based in New Jersey whose staff plans 50 to 80 weddings a year, coast to coast.

The average cost of a wedding in 2009 was $28,385, according to a survey of more than 21,000 U.S. couples conducted by The Knot Inc., a media company devoted to weddings. A wedding's price tag can run a great deal below the average if it's kept casual or a great deal higher—well into six figures—if extravagant. But you and your partner need to decide if this is money well spent or if it's better to cut down on the expense of the wedding so there's more money with which to begin married life. You could, for example, have a budget-conscious wedding at someone's home with buffet tables and a backyard tent.

One strategy for funding a wedding is to plan it well in advance—a year or even two away. This will allow you and your families or whoever's paying for the event to put money away each month and to hunt down discounts on the various items. Setting a date far enough ahead also will help avoid scheduling snafus and other complications that can occur, such as a need to redesign the wedding dress. As always when doing business with vendors—whether caterers, florists, or musicians—get everything in writing. Don't settle for verbal estimates.

For couples who really want a shoestring wedding—including lovebirds who elope—there is the option of getting married simply by obtaining a marriage license and having the ceremony performed by a clergyperson or a court officer. Nevada quickie weddings are an example. A marriage license in Clark County, Nev., where Las Vegas is located, costs $60 as of this printing. A service in a Vegas wedding chapel runs $75 to $200, depending on what frills you add, such as getting hitched by a minister dressed like Elvis. You also have the option of getting married in the county court's civil marriage commissioner's office for a $50 fee.

> If you're hiding your desires, including what you want to purchase for the wedding, even before you're married and are afraid to communicate with each other about expenses that reveals a potential problem in the relationship. There's something underlying the fear of open discussion. You're not working together.
>
> — Samantha Goldberg, wedding planner

As for the honeymoon: The average cost of this post-wedding excursion, industry associations report, is $5,000. Do you really want to go to the place of your dreams if it means paying off the debt for a long time afterward? Or is it wiser to take a long weekend to somewhere nice and enjoy a delayed honeymoon when you can better afford it? These are questions partners must ask.

Engagement and wedding rings also can prove very pricy. In fact, if diamonds are involved, the rings will likely be one of the most expensive outlays in the wedding process. But when it comes to rings, nothing is written in stone, including whether the rings contain the traditional diamonds or other gemstones or are simply metal bands of silver, gold or platinum. Some couples opt for an engagement ring only for the woman. Some couples don't bother with engagement rings at all and invest only in wedding rings.

Couples should consider adjusting expectations for the rings unless they are able or willing to handle their cost. Some people say that an engagement ring's price tag should equal three week's salary; others (within the jewelry industry) suggest two month's salary. A ballpark figure for the cost of the wedding rings is 3 percent of the wedding's budget. Buying a quality ring for a fair price will take legwork. For example, the wise way to search for a diamond ring is to bone up on the grades and values of diamonds, including the 4 C's, which stand for color, clarity, cut, and carat. You also must shop around for a reputable dealer; word of mouth from a satisfied customer you know is a good place to start.

What happens to the engagement ring if the wedding is called off? If a woman refuses to return it to the man who purchased it (or vice-versa), the purchaser can sue in court. Many judges regard an engagement ring as a conditional gift. Some say that condition is marriage; others say the condition is acceptance of a marriage proposal.

Avoid Getting Gouged on the Trip to the Altar

A wedding is meant to be a celebration of a couple's new life. It shouldn't burden that new life with heavy financial debt. Unfortunately, the costs of a wedding can escalate quickly and often without couples even realizing that the price tag is soaring beyond anything they intended.

In the United States, the 2 million-plus weddings each year constitute a $60 billion-a-year industry, according to trade statistics. The wedding business is a racket of sorts; the list of added services and extra features is endless. Some couples hire professional wedding planners to organize and supervise their events; some of the less scrupulous wedding planners get their clients to add on expenses because the planners get a percentage of the total wedding bill—and also may get a share of vendors' profits.

Numerous websites provide free worksheets and even online calculators to help couples budget and track their wedding expenses. In the appendix in the back of this book, you will find a worksheet that will give you an idea of *typical* goods and services to be considered for a wedding. It's entirely up to each couple what they want to include or exclude in their personal budget, so don't be intimidated by the lengthy list. Also know that an endless array of items are available, so this list is hardly exhaustive. The items are broken down into categories that are ranked by a rough percentage of what a category may represent in the entire budget. As always when prudently planning a budget, start by listing the sum of what you have to spend.

Wedding Alarm Bells

Few people have seen as many red flags foretelling a doomed marriage for engaged couples as Samantha Goldberg, a wedding planner based in New Jersey. Since 1992, Goldberg has orchestrated more than 1,000 weddings, for clients ranging from celebrities to everyday brides and grooms.

But whether the couple is seeking a six-figure, lavishly catered wedding or a more humble affair, behavior patterns of the bride- and groom-to-be don't differ according to budget, says Goldberg, a featured host on The Style Network's "Whose Wedding Is It Anyway?" and a regular contributor of wedding articles to magazines, newspapers, and websites.

She can often tell within the first 10 minutes of her initial consultation with the couple whether they are destined to be a happy husband and wife—or headed for great strife. It boils down to how well the bride and groom communicate with each other, sharing their needs and wants. Goldberg is never surprised when she hears that a discordant couple whose wedding she planned ended up divorced.

Planning a wedding can be stressful. It concerns the hot-button issue of a large outlay of money, plus the possible necessities of placating in-laws and friends. Meanwhile, the impending marriage, itself will mean organizing a new household and merging families, with other life-changing events likely on the horizon, such as buying a home and raising children.

Goldberg occasionally witnesses discouraging discord. She'll see a couple sitting across from each other in chairs instead of together on the couch. She'll see one or the other crossing arms. She'll see one party dominate the other—for example, the groom not allowing the bride to express what she wants. "To everything she's saying, he's saying, 'No, we're not doing that,'" Goldberg says.

"In these meetings, each person needs to contribute ideas and let the other party have a say. If you can't plan a wedding without arguing over details and maybe even threatening to call the relationship off—when you're just planning this one day of your life together—you have serious issues to consider. That right there is pretty much your ticket to divorce, even before you get married."

Couples can disguise their relationship as being wonderful, but in fact they lack trust in and respect for each other when they can't cordially come to terms even about the music, the flowers, or how the wedding cake should turn out, Goldberg says.

In relationships where good communication is lacking, one recurrent scenario is the bride making a quick, independent expenditure on her wedding dress, Goldberg says.

"It's pretty typical that when a bride and groom get engaged, the first thing that the bride will do, if she's super anxious, is go out and get the dress. The couple hasn't even really sat down with the parents or whoever's responsible for payments of the entire wedding to really put together a plan of action. When I see brides who go and spend $12,000 on a dress, and they don't have a venue picked out yet or even a date set, that's a super big red flag that tells me she has no respect for the financial situation and what the groom's thoughts will be. Maybe she's afraid that he'll say no. Or maybe she feels she doesn't owe anyone any answers on why she wants to buy an expensive dress. Either way, it shows there's no thought process about the plan of action that's supposed to take place.

"What if the wedding budget is $40,000? Now they've just taken $12,000 out of it for a dress. Once you purchase the dress, you can't return it. And obviously this is a conversation you're not having with the groom, saying, 'How much can we allocate for the apparel for this wedding?'"

Goldberg also has seen grooms make extravagant purchases without consulting their brides, such as one man who charged $5,000 on his credit card to take his groomsmen on a trip to the Caribbean.

"If you're hiding your desires, including what you want to purchase for the wedding, even before you're married and are afraid to communicate with each other about expenses that reveals a potential problem in the relationship. There's something underlying the fear of open discussion. You're not working together."

Some combative couples are able to get a grasp on these issues. "They'll say, 'OK, we need to slow down here and put together a plan. Let's stop this before it gets really out of hand.' If people are going in different directions, arguing about things, not communicating about things that are being purchased, they've got to have that meeting. That one day, the wedding day, may bring a lot of happiness. But the reality of their bad relationship is going to hit them right after the day is done," Goldberg says.

"I've had a bride, on the day of the wedding, call me 10 times. 'The wedding's on. The wedding's off.' Finally she asked me, 'What should I do?' I said, 'I can't answer that for you. Here's the big question I have to ask you: These problems so-and-so has, either you're going to learn to accept them, or you're going to hold off on the marriage and let him figure it out. Or you're going to break up.'

"They got married. A year later, they were in divorce proceedings."

> "The art of living easily as to money is to pitch your scale of living one degree below your means."
> —Sir Henry Taylor

9

Money Choices You Must Make

THE TIME for discussing the big expenses you'll face as a married couple is before you tie the knot, not after. Otherwise, you may just be facing another tremendous expense: a divorce.

Rather than discussions about major expenses being an ordeal, they can serve to bond the two of you together even more tightly. You are creating your financial road map for your marital journey together. That includes where you'll be living, how you'll be living, and who else may be sharing your home in the future (specifically, children).

Keep in mind that basic lifestyle decisions will guide your budget. Even deciding if you'll eat out a lot or take weekend trips will profoundly affect your spending power and likely require tightening in other areas. The chart on page 64 provides information on the expenditures you can expect to have as a couple. It shows the average U.S. consumer expenditures per household by category for 2008 based on U.S. Bureau of Labor Statistics. The average household consisted of 2.5 people with average expenditures of $50,486 and an average pre-tax income of $63,563.

The Home

Housing will account for one-third of your expenditures, according to the Bureau of Labor Statistics. One traditional piece of investment wisdom says that buying a home is a very smart idea. When you pay rent instead of a mortgage, you're not building equity. Also, rents typically rise over time, while a homeowner can lock in a fixed rate of mortgage. The biggest argument for considering home ownership is that, historically, real estate has appreciated at

Average Consumer Expenditures

This pie chart shows average U.S. consumer expenditures per household in various categories. The figures, for 2008, come from the U.S. Bureau of Labor Statistics. Average household expenditures (for 2.5 people) were $50,486; pre-tax income was $63,563.

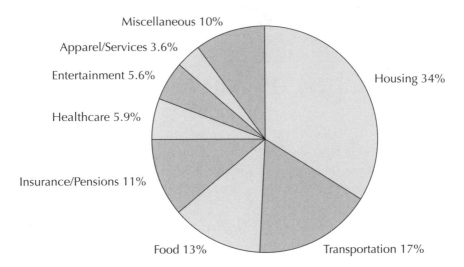

Miscellaneous 10%
Apparel/Services 3.6%
Entertainment 5.6%
Healthcare 5.9%
Insurance/Pensions 11%
Food 13%
Housing 34%
Transportation 17%

about 3 percent more than the inflation rate. Also, the mortgage interest is a tax deduction, as are property taxes and upfront points you pay in the purchase.

But the real-estate market was hit as hard during the recent Great Recession. The classic strategy of buying a home and watching its value consistently rise—building equity for the homeowner—hasn't applied to most properties during the economic downturn. Therefore, the notion that buying a home is a wise investment doesn't necessarily hold true. At least, not in the short term.

If you and your partner are after the traditional American Dream of owning your own home, you have to determine if you're willing and able to come up with the down payment, and whether you're prepared to pay the property taxes, mortgage interest, and homeowners insurance. There's more. Besides covering all the utility fees (and those may include keeping the lawn watered), you'll have to perform maintenance.

And there are still more considerations. If you buy a home, but don't intend to stay in the community for several years (and in a down economy, it might take seven or eight years for your home's price to rise high enough to allow you to at least break even), you face putting the home up for sale in a buyers' market that can leave you with a financial loss—from a depressed sales price and because of agent fees and commissions. If you plan on starting a family and will need a bigger living situation, buying a home that's too small also may not make financial sense.

If you decide to buy, see if you are eligible to receive government assistance on affording a mortgage, such as through Fannie Mae or Freddie Mac, through a first-time homebuyer tax credit, or programs for military veterans. Consider the type of home—house, condominium, or other domicile? And where—in the city, the suburbs, or the country?

Below are the median prices in metropolitan areas for existing single-family homes and for existing condominiums in the first quarter of 2009 in the United States as a whole, and also in four different regions, as reported by the National Association of Realtors. The prices fell in each category over the previous year, reflecting the downturn in the housing market. As an example of monthly costs, the monthly mortgage payment on a $169,000 home with a 6 percent interest rate on a 30-year mortgage would be $1,013.24. The total sum paid over 30 years would be $364,766.40.

Single-family homes:
- Nationwide: $169,000
- Northeast: $235,500
- Midwest: $132,400
- South: $146,600
- West: $237,600

Condominiums:
- Nationwide: $172,800
- Northeast: $220,400
- Midwest: $157,000
- South: $130,000
- West: $174,900

Transportation

Transportation will be another major expense in your budget. The average consumer in our country spends 18 percent of all expenditures on transportation—compared to 13 percent on food—according to the Bureau of Labor

Statistics. Calculating your monthly transportation costs precisely will involve more factors than you may realize, especially if you drive a car.

The American Automobile Association calculated the cost per mile of personal transportation in 2009 for small, midsize, and large sedans, and sports-utility vehicles. The costs are based on driving the vehicle a cumulative 15,000 miles (a ballpark average for a year of driving), and consider both ownership costs (license and registration fees, insurance, depreciation, and financing) and operating costs (fuel at $2.30 a gallon, maintenance, and tires):

- Small sedan: 42.1 cents per mile—$6,312 per year.
- Midsize sedan: 54 cents per mile—$8,105 per year.
- Large sedan: 65.8 cents per mile—$9,870 per year.
- SUV: 68.4 cents per mile—$10,259 per year.

If you're buying a new car, it's usually the second-most expensive purchase you'll make, after a home. The average price of a new car in the United States in 2009 was $28,400, according to the National Automobile Dealers Association. If the car is financed, its ultimate price will be larger. A used car will cost significantly less. A car's purchase price declines steadily each year. An eight-year-old car, regardless of model, generally costs a third to a half as much as the sticker price of when it was new.

Credit Cards and Other Debt and Obligations

It is critical to eliminate negative balances, which can be a slow bleed on your financial welfare. Determine what each of you owes, and plan to retire those balances. Consider consolidating accounts, since too many credit accounts can lower your credit score and hurt you in securing a mortgage. You do want to maintain your individual credit ratings, so keep at least one credit card active in each partner's name.

Make a plan for the regular payment of any child support either partner is required to pay. And, make a plan to repay other loans, such as student loans or outstanding credit-card balances.

Emergency Fund

This fund should contain from three to six months' income in a bank account or money-market fund, so it can be liquidated very easily if need be, such as if one of you loses a job or you suffer some other financial emergency.

Insurance

The rule of thumb is to carry enough insurance to protect your family against events that could create a substantial financial strain. These include high health care costs, an interruption of income because of lost work, a cessation of income because of severe disability or death, physical damage to a home or motor vehicle, or property theft.

Here are the basics on each type of insurance.

Health insurance. This coverage is paramount. With the cost of health care and hospitalization, it is critical to protect yourself with adequate health insurance either through your employer or individually. The main goal is to purchase coverage that has the most attractive combination featuring a low threshold of out-of-pocket costs, a low deductible, and a low premium.

A couple of terms to know: basic hospitalization and major medical. Basic hospitalization insurance covers physician and nursing fees, room and board when you are hospitalized, in-patient or outpatient surgery, X-rays and blood transfusions, drugs and medications, and laboratory tests in or outside the hospital. Major medical insurance covers additional costs outside of basic hospitalization, such as visits to doctors, specialists, and chiropractors, outpatient treatment, drugs, and medical supplies including respirators, wheelchair rentals, and prosthetic devices. Major medical insurance also may cover the costs of X-rays, ambulances, and lab services prescribed by a physician.

Disability insurance. This is the second-most important category of coverage. This ensures you'll be able to receive income in case you are injured and can't continue working. Sometimes the employer offers disability coverage. If not, consider getting a policy that would pay a benefit between 50 and 70 percent of your gross income.

Life insurance. This is especially important if you plan on raising children. A standard amount of coverage equates to five to eight times a person's current annual income. The two general types are term and whole. Term life insurance gives limited protection for a specified period, such as 20 years. The premium—payment—you make each month funds a death benefit. Whole life insurance is like an investment. The monthly premium funds a death benefit, but a portion of the premium goes into a savings account on which the insurance company pays interest. The cash value in this account accumulates tax-deferred (it is only taxed after withdrawn). A tax-free, low-rate loan is possible on this money. The insurance company also will pay a dividend to policyholders, and this money often is used to buy more insurance to reduce the length of time you must pay premiums.

Vehicle insurance is mandated by each state at a minimal level for every automobile, truck, or motorcycle driver. But consider increasing it, if feasible.

Property insurance. Very early in your marriage you should inventory all your belongings. If you received lots of wedding gifts, you'll want to do your inventory before you lose any receipts. Your engagement and wedding rings are probably valuable, so insure them.

(For a more detailed discussion, please consult the chapter on insurance in AIER's book, *How to Avoid Financial Tangles*.)

You can research insurance coverage and rates by going online or calling around to different insurance agencies. You can visit with agents (who sell policies for a specific insurance company), or brokers (independent agents who shop around among different insurers). You'll have to take into account the levels of coverage, the levels of deductibles, the premiums (costs), and the package deals for you and your spouse and any dependents.

You'll also need to choose a financially sound insurer with a good record for paying claims in a timely fashion. The A.M. Best Company is a well-known rating firm. (Membership is free with online registration at www.ambest.com.) The major companies are competitive in their rates for basic coverage of any type. Beware insurance advertised on television or via direct mail. It may seem a bargain, but policies may exclude coverage of certain hazards.

Other Big-Ticket Items

Other big-ticket items can include luxury items—from flat-screen televisions to boats and other expensive toys—as well as vacations and even pets.

The American Society for the Prevention of Cruelty to Animals calculates the annual cost of ownership of comon pets, taking into account food, medical care, litter, toys and treats, license, health insurance, and miscellaneous expenses. The ASPCA also estimates capital costs—including spaying/neutering, leash, living area, and grooming. Here are estimates of first-year costs.

- Small dog: $1,314.
- Medium dog: $1,580.
- Large dog: $1,843.
- Cat: $1,035.
- Rabbit: $1,055.
- Small bird: $270.
- Aquarium fish: $235.

As with all the big-ticket expenses, a failure to consider the cost of pet ownership can strain or bust a budget. And that can land a marriage in the doghouse.

There's one other big-ticket expense we haven't discussed: children. That's the subject of Chapter 14. However, an issue often connected to raising children is appropriate to discuss next: whether both parents will work outside the home.

One- or Two-Paycheck Couple?

With the high cost of living and chronic inflation, two-paycheck couples have become the norm in America. For many families, two incomes are a necessity for sustaining a desired standard of living.

But sometimes the expenses outweigh the benefits. This is especially true when a family has a young child or children. It may be more cost-effective if one of the partners stays home. So unless each partner is content in earning a paycheck and loath to give it up to be a stay-at-home partner or parent, it's worthwhile to compare dollars and cents.

Here's an exercise you should do if you're planning on having children soon after marriage. Or, as the case might be, you may be starting your marriage with one or more young children not yet of school age. Make a list of all the work-related expenses that could be saved if one of the partners stayed home. Items likely will include.

- Vehicle costs (if the vehicle is the mode of work transportation). These would include gasoline, tolls, parking, maintenance, licensing, and insurance. If the vehicle isn't paid off, add in loan payments.
- Bus, train, or cab costs if these are used for transportation.
- Childcare.
- Housekeeping.

- Lunches.
- Work clothes.
- Hair care.
- Work-related dues (such as union fees) and educational expenses.

Another matter to take into account if you intend to be a two-paycheck couple is the strain it can cause on a relationship with both spouses being tired at the end of the day from fighting for a dollar. With two work schedules to consider, it's also harder to match vacation time.

For a couple considering children, the issue of two-paycheck versus one-paycheck is critical. Some family experts say that a child can benefit enormously from having one parent home during those early developmental years. Are both of you on the same page on that issue?

Paycheck Issues Go Beyond Finances

One-paycheck couples face challenges different from two-paycheck couples. There could be added stress from struggling to get by on one paycheck. The stay-at-home partner may resent being stuck doing domestic duty with fewer opportunities to grow personally and professionally outside the parental role.

With maturity comes the ability to tune out the opinions of other people. A wife who works to put her husband through school or to support him while he hunts for a new or better job, may draw criticisms from people who believe the man should be bringing home the bacon. A wife who tends to the home front while the husband works in the salt mines may draw scorn for not developing herself. On the other hand, two-paycheck couples can be ridiculed for being careerist yuppies.

A wise saying is, "What other people think about you is none of your business." It's your life, not theirs.

What this subject of being a one- or two-paycheck couple ultimately boils down to is whether the two of you can decide which arrangement is best for you and whether each of you is content with this decision. The key to financial contentment is having enough money to sustain your desired lifestyle with enough money left over to invest for your futures. You're moving in the right direction if you're doing better than the year before.

> "Some couples go over their budgets very carefully
> every month, others just go over them."
> —Sally Poplin

10
Setting a Budget

SETTING AND sticking to a budget gives you a great deal of control over your financial lives. The right budget will not only keep you living within your means, it can help you direct surplus funds to grow your nest egg. A proper budget will endow you with peace of mind.

Every month across our nation, thousands of charge accounts are revoked, credit cards canceled, vehicles and appliances repossessed, and homes foreclosed on. Sometimes life deals you a nasty hand out of nowhere. You may be the victim of a layoff, divorce, theft, serious injury, or illness. But most financial disasters can be prevented by practicing better budgeting. In fact, most people who declare bankruptcy are fully employed with livable incomes. They simply failed to put a check on their appetite for immediate gratification — and paid a heavy toll for it.

> I'm not resentful about not having two incomes, but a little impatient. She does have a full-time job being a stay-home mom. But there's no way around two incomes. It's much easier than one income.
>
> —Milan, working husband
> with a stay-home wife

In most cases, they abused their available sources of credit. They borrowed their way into insolvency. That's easy to do when credit cards, customer-reward plans, and home-equity lines are peddled in the daily snail mail and spam e-mail. No wonder so many people regard available credit as a form of income. The descent into debt usually happens painlessly. The process is like what a Hemingway character described in the novel *The Sun Also Rises*: "Gradually and then suddenly."

To keep yourself out of the debt trap, you and your partner will need to set up a budgeting system. You will need to agree on where you will keep deposit slips, canceled checks, records of bills, and any important receipts or documents needed for tax records. A filing cabinet is one option.

You will need a place to store bills as they come in and set a time when bills will be paid. You will also need to agree on who is in charge of paying the household bills. Perhaps one of you will handle the routine bills, while the other will oversee the investments.

Sit down together and figure out the budget that you will have after getting married. This will help you focus very clearly on how you will make your marriage financially viable. A handy way to determine what your budget will be is to estimate your yearly incomes and expenses.

Determine Your Income

Make three columns on a piece of paper. In the column on the left write income, and beneath it, on separate lines, write wages, investment income, and other income. (This last category can represent sources such as alimony, child support, trust payments, and rent from properties.) In the second column write monthly and in the third column put yearly. The work sheet will look like the one below.

You and your partner can determine your respective incomes and then add them together. The figures should be for *net income* (meaning, after taxes).

Income	Monthly	Yearly
(His) Wages	$2,618	$31,416
(His) Investment income	$42	$504
(His) Other income	$0	$0
(Her) Wages	$3,326	$39,912
(Her) Investment income	$0	$0
(Her) Other income	$0	$0
TOTAL	$5,986	$71,832

Determine Your Expenses

Next set your budget. Below is a table showing the average expenditures for two-person households in 2007-2008. The figures (rounded out) come from the Bureau of Labor Statistics.

If either of you has fluctuating income—for example, if you own a business, or work on commission—you will need to take special care in setting a budget.

Expenditures	Monthly	(Total)	Annual	%/Total

FOOD
  Food at home
  Food away from home
	
	$245
	$261
		$506	$6,073	11.6%

Alcoholic beverages		$56	$676	1.3%

HOUSING
  Shelter
  Utilities, fuels, and public
   services
  Household operations,
   housekeeping
  Furnishings and equipment
	
	$991
	$252
	
	$100
	$180
		$1,522	$18,264	35.2%

APPAREL AND SERVICES		$173	$2,073	4.0%

TRANSPORTATION
  Vehicle purchases (net outlay)
  Gasoline and motor oil
  Other vehicle expenses
  Public transportation
	
	$351
	$227
	$222
	$48
		$847	$10,169	19.5%

HEALTH CARE
  Health insurance
  Drugs
  Medical services and supplies
	
	$80
	$17
	$49
		$146	$1,750	3.4%

ENTERTAINMENT		$236	$2,831	5.4%
PERSONAL CARE PRODUCTS/SERVICES		$54	$642	1.2%
EDUCATION AND READING		$96	$1,152	2.2%
TOBACCO PRODUCTS AND SMOKING SUPPLIES		$28	$331	0.6%
PERSONAL INSURANCE AND PENSIONS		$549	$6,583	12.6%
MISCELLANEOUS		$146	$1,751	3.4%
Total expenditures	$4,358		$52,295	100%

Two special practices are in order when you keep your financial records.

- Conservatively estimate your average income for the year ahead. Take into account what you'll have to subtract from this income—including regular business expenses and business taxes. Come up with your net (not gross) income. Then divide this figure by 12. This will yield you a monthly average.
- Keep your business expenses separate from your household expenses. Remember that business-expense reimbursements, such as checks for gas mileage, should not be considered family income.

Now you and your partner must itemize your expenses. Estimate how much you'll spend together on the various items in the table on the opposite page.

A Few Words on Investing

A few words are in order regarding investing—which could also take up a portion of your budget. (The pensions in the Personal insurance and pensions line is a form of investing.) As mentioned earlier, it's prudent to have from three to six months' income in a bank account or money-market fund as an emergency fund that can be liquidated very easily if needed, in case one of you loses a job or some other financial emergency arises.

When it comes to saving and investing, there's an old concept known as paying yourself first. If you can save between 5 and 10 percent of your weekly or monthly income, then you're setting aside money to grow for your future, which includes your retirement.

One Couple's Story

Milan and Monica, married Owls introduced in Chapter 1, went from a two-income to a single-income household after their son was born. Monica became a stay-at-home parent, while Milan became the sole breadwinner with his business as an advertising art director and website designer.

Milan's stress level has increased from this arrangement, and he yearns for his wife to return to earning a full-time paycheck. Their son is approaching preschool age, which will help the family return to a two-income arrangement. This will be a relief for Monica as well—not only for the increase in cash flow, but because of the emotional liability of not earning money herself.

"She can't wait to get a job again," Milan says. "She doesn't like feeling like she has no power about how our money is spent. She'll think, 'Can we buy this?' and think she needs my authorization. She really doesn't, but feels like she does."

"In the beginning, when we had our son, my focus on making money went

Expenditures	Monthly	(Total)	Annual	%/Total

FOOD
  Food at home
  Food away from home				

Alcoholic beverages				

HOUSING
  Shelter
  Utilities, fuels, and public
    services
  Household operations,
    housekeeping
  Furnishings and equipment				

APPAREL AND SERVICES				

TRANSPORTATION
  Vehicle purchases (net outlay)
  Gasoline and motor oil
  Other vehicle expenses
  Public transportation				

HEALTH CARE
  Health insurance
  Drugs
  Medical services and supplies				

ENTERTAINMENT				
PERSONAL CARE PRODUCTS/ SERVICES				
EDUCATION AND READING				
TOBACCO PRODUCTS, SMOKING SUPPLIES				
PERSONAL INSURANCE AND PENSIONS				
MISCELLANEOUS				
Total expenditures				100%

by the wayside," Monica says. "My focus was on how to take care of this baby. But then about a year ago, I started to reflect, 'OK, maybe I need to re-launch my career again because I've always been self-sufficient. I've been working since I was 15 and always had my own money.' I started thinking, 'OK, he's the breadwinner right now, and I'm not contributing and I'm spending money. And I feel almost guilty that I'm spending his money on personal things, such as facials, the night out with the girls, buying clothes, buying shoes, lipstick.' To make my own money is really important to me."

"I'm not resentful about not having two incomes, but a little impatient," Milan says. "She does have a full-time job being a stay-home mom. But there's no way around two incomes. It's much easier than one income."

"Too many people spend money they haven't earned, to buy things they don't want, to impress people they don't like."

—Will Smith

11

Spending the Wealth— His and Her Accounts

JUST BECAUSE you're getting married doesn't mean the two of you suddenly will lose your personalities as individuals. You'll each still have your own needs and desires—including ways of thinking about money.

You each should enjoy a measure of personal control over the family funds. A great strategy—one you should agree to before the marriage—is to set up *three* checking accounts for handling household income.

Separate but Equal Accounts

The first account will be the joint, or House, account. This is the account you'll use to cover all your household expenses plus the money you put toward investments. The other two accounts are the His account and Her account. Into each of these two accounts goes a specified and equal sum each month, regardless of who brings in the money or earns more. In a marriage, you are equal partners.

How *much* should this total sum be? It can be the amount of money left over each month after all the other budget items are met, including funding investments. Or it can be the leftover money up to a certain amount (with the remainder put, perhaps, into savings or investments).

"Definitely expect there will be some hashing out of what belongs in each fund," says marriage and family therapist Kevin Roth.

The money in the His account is up to the discretion of the husband. The money in the Her account is up to the discretion of the wife. Certain budgetary items may fall into a gray area and end up—by prior agreement between the two spouses—being covered by one or the other partner. The wife may be a big fan of the *Sunday New York Times*, for example, but the husband may be only interested in getting his news each morning online on his home page. In this case, the wife could agree to pay for the *Times* subscription out of Her account.

And let's say the husband, bless him, is still interested in driving his flashy sports car and is resistant to having his wife get behind the wheel. The pricy insurance premium to cover that car far exceeds the rate for his wife's hybrid. So it's agreed that he'll pay the difference of the two rates out of the His account.

Let's say the wife has exquisite taste in shoes and enjoys increasing her collection several times a year. Rather than include these splurges in the monthly budget, she pays for this out of the Her account. Ditto her membership at the yoga studio. Ditto his softball team gear and league dues, and bankroll for poker tournaments.

> The House account is something you agree upon as a couple. It gives you the freedom to buy that comic book if you want it, or a pair of shoes, and not have to sneak it into the house and worry your spouse will say, "Why didn't you discuss this with me?" It's healthy for a relationship.
>
> —Amy, who set up a House account with her husband

What may seem a frivolous expense to one partner may be emotionally important to the other. To be sure, the freedom of each partner to spend money according personal wishes or whims is vital to a marriage's success. The His and Her accounts are safety valves.

"These accounts are a way of preventing resentment from building," Roth says.

One Couple's Story

When Amy and Arthur got married, they were in their 40's and each had been previously married, with children from those marriages. Amy and Arthur were used to their separate ways. "I had my account, and he had his account," says Amy, a photographer. "We just kept separate accounts for a long time."

She moved to Las Vegas to live with Arthur, an editor and writer who owned a home. They acknowledged he was the better money manager and should handle the bills. Every two weeks he'd add up bills and divvy up expenses.

Arthur wrote checks for the bills on his own account. "I'd write him a check for paying the household bills," Amy says. "It started getting to the point where I thought he was asking me for too much money and he started thinking I was hiding money. It was causing conflict in our relationship."

The solution? They agreed on one sum that she'd deposit each month into Arthur's checking account, and the remainder would be hers to spend as she wished. This system—in effect, a House account and a Her account—was Amy's idea, Arthur says. "I was quite surprised when she came up with the idea."

His checking account has no firewall preventing Amy's access. It is linked to a joint savings account. However, Amy's own account remains in her name only.

"I haven't any idea what goes on in there," Arthur says. "I know she isn't stashing away big chunks of money because I trust her."

The new system has proved effective.

"It's made a huge difference—not only with handling the bills and the stress, but the trust issue and emotional factor with the relationship itself," Amy says. "We're both happier, and we don't have these thoughts in our heads, 'Well, she's not giving me enough,' or, 'He's asking too much.'"

The money they put in the House account covers the mortgages on their home plus a rental property they own, power and utility bills, home and car insurance, and payments on joint credit cards. They own separate vehicles and therefore keep car payments separate. Similarly, they maintain separate retirement funds and pay their individual business bills separately.

Besides covering living expenses together, they save together for trips or other big-ticket items. When the rental market bounces back, and they start enjoying a revenue stream from their rental property, which they co-own, "It will probably go into a joint savings account, to use as retirement," Amy says.

She buys fabric for her quilting hobby with her own money, and he buys his collectible comic books with surplus money in the House checking account, and they never question each other.

Overall, their account system preserves sanity in their marriage, Amy says. It keeps resentment—a curse of many marriages—from building.

"The House account is something you agree upon as a couple," Amy says.

"It gives you the freedom to buy that comic book if you want it or a pair of shoes, and not have to sneak it into the house and worry your spouse will say, 'Why didn't you discuss this with me?' It's healthy for a relationship."

Arthur agrees. Honesty, openness—transparency—are key to a relationship's health and survival, he says. "After all, eventually secrets will come out, and that can cause a huge problem. As my grandma used to say, 'It all comes out in the wash.'"

> "Some debts are fun when you are acquiring them, but none are fun when you set about retiring them."
> —Ogden Nash

12

The Curse of Debt

YOUNG COUPLES often face debt traps. Three of the most typical are student loans, car loans, and credit-card balances.

For people in the early stages of building careers, where income is relatively small, paying off these debts in full seems as arduous as the mythical Sisyphus pushing a boulder up a mountain. The good news is that, unlike hapless Sisyphus, the task can be accomplished instead of having the burden continually roll back down.

As you prepare yourself for marriage, you need to think about your and your partner's current debt load—and how you are addressing these burdens.

The following information will serve you well now—and after you marry.

Retiring Debt Is a Good Place to Start

While saving and investing for retirement is critical to fashioning a sound financial plan, often it makes more sense to retire first debts that chronically consume your income through high-interest payments. Simple mathematics proves this point. Say you have $100 left over from monthly expenses. If it earns 8 percent annually in an investment, you will have $108 at the end of a year. If you are paying 12 percent on a $100 credit-card balance, you will owe $112 at the end of a year. Better to pay off that balance with your $100 surplus.

It's often easy to ignore a shaky financial situation and just continue to get by month to month, but that's a prescription for remaining in debt and falling further behind. It also robs you of one of your greatest assets when you are young: making time work for you by having your assets grow and compound through interest and earnings.

Here are warning signs you should heed.

- You're making only the minimum payment (meaning the interest) on a credit-card bill each month.
- You're using one credit card to pay off another.
- You've maxed out the limit on a card.
- You're using credit cards to pay for groceries, gasoline, or other necessities.

You may need to recommit yourself to sticking to a budget and perhaps revise your budget to tighten up spending. Analyze your expenditures of the past year. You can survey checkbooks or view expenditures in online statements, determine what was unnecessary, frivolous, or perhaps too pricy, and then figure out how to avoid such waste in the future.

There are so many ways to trim one's outlay of cash. You can brown-bag it to work instead of buying lunch. You can make more meals at home rather than eating out. You can buy more produce and grains and fewer processed foods. You can clip coupons. You can avoid long-distance phone calls and endless texting. You can find cheaper calling plans—or bundle plans for Internet access, telephone, and cable use. You can find cheaper forms of entertainment than going to high-ticket concerts or ball games. Finally, you can resolve to bite the bullet for a time by giving up certain luxuries: a health-club membership, guitar lessons, a magazine subscription, and so on.

If you're trying to pay down a large amount of credit-card debt, you can consider debt consolidation—rolling all your balances into one big loan. Simple math will determine if this is wise. If the consolidated payment is less than the sum of all your payments, it makes sense. You can start chipping away at the principal—paying off more than the minimum payment each month—until the debt is shrunk and then gone.

If you realize you're treading financial water or slowly drowning and can't seem to get your nose above the surface, consider contacting a credit-counseling service. Many of these agencies are nonprofit, but it's buyer beware because some of them charge hidden fees or may urge you to make contributions. Some are largely funded by credit issuers, and their advice may be meant to benefit lenders instead of borrowers.

Places to start searching for a helpful credit-counseling organization are through the U.S. Cooperative Extension Service, your local university, your bank, or a local consumer-protection agency.

Do be wary of advertisements on television or the Internet, in newspapers, or the telephone book that promise debt relief. They may simply be offering services to help you declare bankruptcy. Bankruptcy should be employed only as a last resort because bankruptcy information stays on your credit report for 10 years—which can make it difficult for you to get credit, buy a home, obtain life insurance, or even get a job.

Beware of Risky Mortgages

Recent history provides a great lesson to first-time homebuyers.

The so-called subprime mortgage crisis that struck in 2007 and triggered the worldwide recession was caused in part by the loose credit policies that financial institutions offered to U.S. homebuyers with weak ("subprime") financial positions. The housing market in the years leading up the crisis was strong, with prices continually increasing. That led many consumers to take on mortgages with payments they could afford over the short term, but which would involve much higher payments after a period of time.

> We did almost everything right—saved 30 percent of our income, invested aggressively enough for our age. Our biggest mistake was that when things got bad, we didn't communicate.
>
> —Louise, whose marriage was threatened after the subprime recession ravaged her husband's income and their investment portfolio

Many subprime borrowers believed that with the increase in value of their homes in the hot market, they would be able to refinance their homes at better rates in the years ahead. In other words, the subprime mortgages would allow them to become homeowners. They could then realize a relatively quick appreciation in value of their home and use that new wealth to obtain a mortgage at better terms. Some also may have considered selling their homes at a profit.

Two of these types of subprime loans were for interest-only mortgages and for adjustable-rate mortgages (ARMs). Interest-only mortgages allow for monthly payments on a loan's interest (with no portion of the principal included) for a specified number of years. After that period, though, the payment rate jumps significantly, covering both the principal and interest.

ARMs have rates tied to the financial market. If interest rates rise, the cost of a mortgage rises. The initial rate on an ARM is usually lower than that of a traditional fixed-rate mortgage. This means that borrowers who couldn't quality for fixed-rate mortgages could qualify for ARMs. Approximately four out of five U.S. mortgages to subprime borrowers in the period preceding the subprime recession were ARMs. When U.S. housing prices began dropping in 2006, refinancing became more difficult, and ARMs began resetting at higher rates. That precipitated an epidemic of mortgage defaults and home foreclosures, with a plunge in the value of securities backed by subprime mortgages and held by financial firms. The dominoes began toppling. Banks lost capital, credit tightened around the world, and a severe recession resulted.

The easy availability of subprime lending has vanished as of this writing, and governmental regulation of financial markets may limit the access to these risky mortgages in the future. But if these mortgage vehicles manage to reappear in different forms, recognize them as too risky for a young couple to accept. It's much wiser for would-buy homebuyers to adequately save for this big investment, to perhaps enlist the help of family members to make the down payment, and to take on a fixed-rate mortgage for which they qualify.

One Couple's Story

Even partners who are money savvy can commit basic blunders that prove costly to their financial security—and threaten their marriage.

Louise has more than 10 years experience in the credit industry. She had worked as a paralegal for a bankruptcy lawyer and as a business credit consultant for Experian, the giant credit-information group. She was certified to underwrite Fannie Mae loans for homebuyers, and she writes a column for a website geared to people with mortgage-credit problems.

Her husband, Mark, is a mortgage loan officer who'd worked nine years for a large, well-known residential builder in the company's division that financed mortgages. Mark's niche was high-end financing and construction loans. Working on commission, he earned $300,000 a year.

Louise and Mark were in their 40's—first marriage for him, second for her—and worked together on their financial goals. They were making solid financial moves. Their beautiful home in an upscale subdivision was increasing in equity as the housing market soared. They also owned a buildable lot in another subdivision. They saved for Louise's daughter's college fund. Mark planned to retire at 55. Louise enjoyed her work, but figured she'd quit if she ever got tired or bored. They scrupulously put 30 percent of Mark's earnings into a deferred-compensation plan set up by his employer. The money in this account would not be taxed until it was withdrawn. The couple invested the deferred-comp money in mutual funds.

They were enjoying the good life. Then in 2007, the subprime credit crisis hit—a large domino that triggered the recession. "When the entire toilet is flushed, everything goes down," Louise says. "The real estate market tanked at the same time as the stock market tanked, and my husband's business dropped nearly to zero." Mark's company closed its mortgage division, and he went to work for another large lender. The deferred-comp plan ended, and the money in it immediately became taxable as income earned—incurring a $120,000 bite from the Internal Revenue Service.

"So we lost $120,000 off the top in taxes," Louise says. "And our home equity went away. All the funds we had been saving and saving and should have been able to rely on in a crisis went away. In less than 18 months, we lost $1.1 million in value. There was $600,000 in real estate, and over $400,000 in value in mutual funds."

Contributing to the constant hemorrhage was Mark's drought in earnings. "He told me that the clients were coming in," Louise says. "I assumed business was coming in, and he was closing deals." But he wasn't closing deals. The clients who came in ended up falling out. He kept that a secret."

Mark continued paying the bills by borrowing against the retirement fund he'd rolled over to his new employer and by selling the couple's stock even though prices had plunged. In this way, most of their retirement investments disappeared.

"And then one day I got the statements in," Louise says. "There was one set of statements that I hadn't seen, that he probably didn't dump in my in-box. By the time I found we were really down, he'd gone nine months without making any money."

The couple separated for a period. After they reconciled, they reviewed their situation and how they'd gotten there.

"The one thing we did do right is we didn't sit there and blame each other," Louise says. "My philosophy is you make the best decision you can at the time. I don't like it that he pulled money out of our retirement fund. But we drew up a plan and worked as a team. We sat down and went through everything, every line item, and we're working on cutting back."

Louise has sold her Lotus sports car to replenish their stock investments, and is negotiating a short sale on the vacant lot of which the value dropped to $150,000 less than what they owed.

"Our biggest mistake was that when things got bad, we didn't communicate," Louise says. "Our second biggest mistake was having no emergency money that was not invested in funds and stocks.

"The fact is we lost $1 million and didn't spend it on anything fun. And it almost cost us our marriage, too. With some work and sacrifice we are pulling it back together and will be OK. Even financial experts and mortgage-savvy people can find themselves in trouble. It only takes one mistake."

"If you would be wealthy, think of saving as well as getting."
—Benjamin Franklin

13

Setting a Financial Plan

IT MAY be difficult, as you live in the moment, for you and your partner to look ahead occasionally toward that distant period called the Golden Years—meaning retirement. But when it comes to your journey together toward that distant time, the two of you should harbor similar goals.

"Those who fail to plan, plan to fail," the old saying goes. The last thing you'll want to face is a double-whammy: advanced age and impoverishment.

One general goal to set is the age at which you each plan to retire. Another goal is deciding how much money you'll need to save or invest that will allow you to retire at the age you've chosen.

Setting these goals are worthy mental exercises, but should not be considered as set in stone. After all, the economy is unpredictable, and financial markets are volatile. Besides, you never know what the future holds in store for you in terms of employment, health, and circumstances. Even the most focused, disciplined, and optimistic among us have relatively limited control over their lives.

But one thing you *can* take charge of is to practice *good financial habits*. That's the key.

Practicing Good Financial Habits

Good habits, financial advisor Mackenzie Waggaman says, can get you through just about anything. "If your goal is to be in good physical shape, you must eat right, sleep right, and exercise right. Otherwise you won't be healthy. Good habits give you the potential to obtain goals."

When it comes to getting in financial shape, Waggaman says, you don't necessarily need a high income to make a killing in real estate or the stock market or get some other windfall that will allow you to attain a comfortable financial footing. Most important is practicing sound financial habits. These habits fall into four general categories.

1. Keeping yourself from getting mired in debt.
2. Building up a financial reserve.
3. Maintaining adequate insurance.
4. Having your money work for you through prudent investments.

Keeping yourself from getting mired in debt was the subject of Chapter 12. Maintaining adequate insurance was discussed in Chapter 9. How to build up a financial reserve? Start saving on a regular basis—such as putting a bit of money aside each month or even each week.

"When it comes to young couples investing, just putting cash in the bank is a great habit to get into," Waggaman says. "It's boring and not exciting like buying a commodity future. But it's much wiser and more prudent. Investing should not be exciting. Investing is not an Xtreme sport. It's more like bowling than bungee jumping. It's more like chess than poker."

You can begin developing this investment habit with a simple step: Carve out time for learning about investing. The avenues for investing are endless, so when it comes to buying shares in the stock market or investing in any other financial market—whether it's real estate or commodities such as natural gas or gold—a bit of homework will be required before jumping in.

Waggaman says it's imperative for couples to take the time to educate themselves about investing. "A marriage license should be like a driver's license—the partners should be able to pass tests," he declares. "And one of those tests should be financial literacy."

A Few Basics of Investing

One problem encountered by new investors is the tremendous volume of information available about investing. There are newsletters and brochures, online articles, and courses at community colleges. Much of this information is provided by financial firms or brokers. The financial industry is sales oriented. So keep in mind that information from firms or brokers is geared toward selling stocks or other securities for which the sellers receive fees or commissions.

Sifting through information for solid, unbiased advice takes time and effort. One option is taking an inexpensive subscription to American Investment Services' monthly *Investment Guide*, which covers investment theory and reports on financial markets and what they mean to individual investors. AIS is a subsidiary wholly owned by the American Institute for Economic Research (this book's publisher). Every three months AIS's *Investment Guide* contains charts of model portfolios based on the individual's investment risk, plus a list of low-cost mutual funds available to all investors. AIS analysis is based on unbiased research by the nonprofit, independent AIER.

There are some basic principles to sound investing. One is to invest for the long term. You'll want to take advantage of the magic of compound interest. Another basic principle is investing on a regular schedule— such as setting aside money each week or month. An easy way to make regular payments into an investment is through automatic electronic withdrawals from your checking account into a savings account or investment account.

> Good habits give you the potential to attain goals. When it comes to young couples investing, just putting cash in the bank is a great habit to get into. It's boring and not exciting like buying a commodity future. But investing is not an Xtreme sport. It's more like bowling than bungee jumping. It's more like chess than poker.
>
> —Mackenzie Waggaman, financial advisor

Basic investment strategies differ according to one's age, the total number of years one has with which to invest before retirement, and one's appetite and ability to sustain risk. For people with an investing career of 25 or more years, putting money in the stock market is a time-tested road for investing for retirement. The trick is in spreading the risk among stocks in different industries or funds, such as growth and income funds or an international fund.

Each investor's situation is unique, and many variables must be considered. But it all boils down to understanding risk and how much you're willing to accept. A large number of risk-tolerance questionnaires are posted on the Internet. You can find them instantly by typing the key words "risk," "tolerance," and "questionnaire" into a search engine. These quizzes typically ask 10 or so questions and require only a few minutes to fill out. After you submit your answers, your risk-tolerance score will be calculated immediately. The score will tell you whether your tolerance is low, below average, average/moderate, above average, or high.

A Few More Tips on Investing

Take advantage of tax-deferred accounts. These include 401(k)s, and individual retirement accounts (IRAs). They allow the money you put into such an account to accumulate without having tax bites taken out of it every year. The difference over time is enormous. Here's an example from AIER's book, *How to Avoid Financial Tangles*:

If you invest $1,000 in an account earning an 8 percent rate of return per year, after 10 years you'll have $2,160. But if your annual earnings are taxed as income, and your marginal tax rate is 28 percent, your after-tax return will be reduced to 5.76 percent a year, and after 10 years you'll have only $1,750. That's 20 percent less than in the tax-free account. And after 20 years, the tax-free account would be worth $4,660—compared to the $3,065 in the taxable account.

Diversify. Don't put all your eggs in one basket. Spread the risk of your investments by choosing investments that aren't all affected by the same financial market conditions. A typical portfolio is divided among three major asset categories—stocks (ownership in companies), bonds (which earn interest as loans to governments or companies), and cash equivalents (such as currency). A vast variety of investments exists in each of these categories. When it comes to stocks, there are large-caps and small-caps, domestic and foreign, value and growth. You can invest in small companies that stand a chance for enormous growth or large companies with long track records of stability. You also can invest in index funds that hold a mix of stocks.

The more risk you take, such as putting money in stocks rather than bonds or cash, or in other markets such as commodities (examples: gold or oil), the more you increase your chance for a greater return. Your timetable for investing will affect this decision. With fewer years before planned retirement and less time to ride out short-term market fluctuations, you'll want less risk.

Keep expenses low. Money managers are happy to take 1.5 percent (or some other figure) from you each year. Mutual funds also take bites from you, as do brokers who take a fee per transaction. You may decide to go instead with low-cost index funds or manage your own affairs through a discount-brokerage house.

A list of investment primers from the American Institute for Economic Research is contained in the appendix of this book.

Absorbing valuable advice on the steps you should take to manage your finances and invest wisely and actually agreeing to a specific course of action with your partner are two different matters. If either of you feels unsure about setting up an investment portfolio, consider consulting a financial advisor. Seek out a professional with at least 10 years of experience. A referral from a friend or associate is preferable.

Avoiding Financial Predators

"A fool and his money are soon parted," said the English writer Thomas Tusser in the 16th century. Plenty of predators lurk out there hoping that you'll be one of the 21st century fools.

Besides investing regularly and wisely to get your money to work for you, you want to prevent your money from working for someone else. To protect your hard-earned income, avoid these current scams.

Phishing. Scammers e-mail messages that appear to be from legitimate companies, such as banks or websites. A message may say that the website is working to enhance security or prevent fraud, or needs to update your account information. Do not reconfirm your identity by entering personal information such as a Social Security or credit-card number. Never provide this information over the Internet unless you were the one to initiate contact.

ID theft. Your Social Security number is the key to your bank accounts, credit report, and other sensitive information. While financial institutions and employers need your number for wage and tax reporting, and landlords or utility companies may seek it for a credit check on you, giving it out to others can prove dangerous.

Pay attention to billing cycles, and review account statements to see if there are any odd charges. A bill for something you never bought or a letter or call from a bill collector regarding a purchase you never made are obvious red flags.

Check your credit history once a year to make sure that an ID thief hasn't ruined your credit. As mentioned in Chapter 2, you can obtain free reports online at www.annualcreditreport.com.

Credit-card theft. Never give out your credit-card digits or other personal information over the telephone or on websites unless you have initiated the contact. And only provide personal information to websites with a secure server. These sites have a locked padlock icon at the bottom of the browser page. URLs that begin with "https" are secure.

Tear up prescreened credit-card offers you get in the mail, so no one else can fill them out in your name.

Password theft. Use original user passwords for websites, e-mail accounts, and cell-phone accounts, and don't use the same password for each account. Change your passwords periodically.

A Financial Plan for Beginning Investors

The ultimate goal of a financial plan is financial security. This security is based upon being free of debt, having liquid assets (such as cash in the bank) for an emergency reserve and for investing, and making investments that steadily grow one's estate.

Financial advisor Mackenzie Waggaman's essential steps for the beginning investor.

Create liquidity. This means to have extra cash available. Figure out what you're earning and what your expenses are, and live way below your means. "Don't think about investing until you've got lots of cash in the bank."

Eliminate debt. If you're in debt, get out of debt before investing. Otherwise you're steadily losing money by paying interest and possibly other charges. One type of debt, however, that you don't need to pay off right away is a home mortgage as long as it's within your means to carry it.

Have an emergency fund. Build up an emergency fund of cash or certificates of deposit (CDs), in the bank. Some experts recommend having a fund equivalent to three to six months' income to guard against ruin from losing a job or another crisis.

Make tax-deferred investments. Once debts have been paid and an emergency fund saved, cash left over after meeting the monthly budget can be invested. Among the optimal places for investing are tax-deferred retirement accounts. These include 401(k)s (offered by some employers), Simplified Employee Pension, or SEP, plans (available to self-employed people and to employees of small companies offering SEPs), and simple IRAs or Roth IRAs (which can be opened at brokerages, including discount brokerages). These accounts allow assets to grow steadily. Some 401(k) plans include matching dollars from employers.

Find a discount brokerage. After maxing out contributions to tax-deferred retirement accounts, investors can consider getting an account with a discount brokerage. Such brokerages charge low fees for transactions and allow investors easy access to making their own buys and trades. This would be a taxable account—meaning investment gains are subject to tax, but losses can be included on tax returns.

> "The easiest way for your children to learn about
> money is for you not to have any."
> —Katharine Whitehorn

14
Family Planning

CHILDREN ARE the light of most parents' lives, but they don't come cheap. Not only are they the No. 1 responsibility in a parent's life, they also are one of—if not the—biggest expense in a household budget.

The U.S. Department of Agriculture's Center for Nutrition Policy and Promotion provides estimates of the annual cost of raising a child. Its calculations factor in each child's age, the number of children in the household, the family's income level, whether it's a one- or two-parent household, and in which region the family lives. The calculation includes housing, food, transportation, clothing, health care, child care, education, and other costs.

A sampling of these calculations is on page 96. The figures are based on national, not regional, averages for 2007, the latest year data was available as of this printing.

None of the figures include saving for the child's college expenses. According to the College Board, in 2008-09 the average cost in the United States for tuition and fees at a public, four-year institution of higher education was $6,585. At a private institution, it was $25,143. Both figures represented more than a 5 percent increase over the year before. Living expenses were not included in the totals.

Leaving Work Is another Budget Impact

A husband and wife will likely see a drop in income during a pregnancy if the wife works but must take maternity leave. The two also may consider one or the other taking time off from work after the child is born. Either spouse is protected from losing a job if the wife gets pregnant. The Family and Medical

Leave Act requires that employers offer employees 12 weeks of unpaid leave with a continuation of health benefits in the case of a pregnancy.

Some experts recommend that a mother take three to five months leave from work to foster bonding with the baby. Each situation is unique, however. And a couple may face another big decision—having one or the other parent become a full-time parent for a number of months or years.

Annual Expenditures on Children

Two-parent household, earning less than $45,800
- One child, age 1: $9,709.
- One child, age 10: $9,858.
- One child, age 16: $10,924.
- Two children, ages 1 and 3: $15,850.
- Two children, ages 10 and 12: $16,780.
- Two children, ages 16 and 17: $17,620.
- Three children, ages 10, 12, and 16: $19,704.

Two-parent household, earning $45,800 to $77,100
- One child, age 1: $13,590.
- One child, age 10: $13,553.
- One child, age 16: $14,917.
- Two children, ages 1 and 3: $22,240.
- Two children, ages 10 and 12: $22,620.
- Two children, ages 16 and 17: $24,060.
- Three children, ages 10, 12, and 16: $26,681.

Two-parent household, earning more than $77,100
- One child, age 1: $20,200.
- One child, age 10: $19,815.
- One child, age 16: $21,700.
- Two children, ages 1 and 3: $32,960.
- Two children, ages 10 and 12: $32,790.
- Two children, ages 16 and 17: $35,000.
- Three children, ages 10, 12, and 16: $38,723.

All these decisions will have a huge bearing on the household budget. The question of whether they want children is standard among young couples considering marriage. If the answer is yes, how many children also is a common and important question.

Along with it should be a third question: How do we intend to afford this child or children?

Staying Home with the Baby—Not Just a Money Issue

When it comes to deciding on who will stay home with a newborn or infant, each household's situation is different. Some couples, for example, have a network of extended family or friends that can help with tending to a baby's needs. In all cases, when a new addition to the family arrives, the parents should

> The stay-at-home person may need to go back to work for her or his self-esteem, or for the sanity of being around other adults. It just doesn't have to be a financial decision alone.
> — Kevin Roth, marriage and family therapist

be prepared to be flexible when it comes to prior expectations.

The 18th-century Scottish poet Robert Burns famously observed, "The best-laid schemes o' mice an' men/Gang aft a-gley." Translation: No matter how well you think out a plan, that plan can go awry.

"There are women who get married and can hardly wait to become a mother. But then they find that being home all the time with kids drives them nuts," says Kevin Roth. "Other women are more careerist, but discover that full-time mothering is great and fulfilling." And some men, too, find satisfaction in being "Mr. Moms," a reversal of the traditional parenting role.

The length of being a full-time, stay-at-home parent should vary with a family's financial considerations and also the parents' emotional needs, which must not be underestimated, Roth says. "If the stay-at-home parent needs to get away from child-rearing responsibilities to preserve mental health or needs more time to earn money, those are vital considerations.

"The stay-at-home person may need to go back to work for her or his self-esteem, or for the sanity of being around other adults. I would take that into account. For example, the stay-home mother may have fears about her identity being tied to being a mom. A lot of times that brings up insecurities. A woman who has been a professional in the workforce and switches to being a full-time mom may lose self-confidence. She may need to resume her career.

"The same is true if you're a house husband. Plus, there are gender stereotypes to consider. If I took my kids out to the park or to McDonald's, I'd definitely have a tape running in my head, feeling that people would be silently questioning why I was not at work. Also, it's easier for a woman to strike up a conversation with another woman at the park. It's different for a man. She'd wonder whether I was hitting on her or just socializing."

The decision on who stays home with an infant, for how long, and whether it's full-time or part-time, involves many factors and layers of needs, Roth says. "It just doesn't have to be a financial decision alone or solely a parental decision alone."

> "What counts in making a happy marriage
> is not so much how compatible you are,
> but how you deal with incompatibility."
> —Leo Tolstoy

15
Resolving Monetary Conflict

THAT A marriage takes work is a cliché. When it comes to money talk, just as in raising the children or addressing romantic needs, effective communication is the key.

If you're considering marriage, you must be certain you're capable of effective communication with your partner, including talking about money issues as they arise.

This serious talk should not be precipitated spontaneously, but be conducted in the proper environment and time. It should not be done in bed or at the breakfast table—or when one of you is exhausted after a long day at the office, cleaning house, or doing yard work. Set aside time for it, and conduct it in a quiet setting where you won't be interrupted.

As mentioned in Chapter 6, men in general aren't the best communicators of their emotions, while women like to talk about their troubles. But communicating about money matters is critical to your relationship's health and success.

The bottom line in fostering good communication is remembering to respect the other's feelings and opinions.

Tips for Aiding a Meeting of Minds

Start money conversations by conveying what you are feeling and why. The order of points, says marriage therapist Kevin Roth, is *fact*, *thought*, *feeling*, and *request for change*. For example, "You went out and bought a car and didn't ask me. Maybe you don't respect me or think my feelings matter. When you act like that, I get hurt. When you're considering a big purchase, I want you to talk with me about it beforehand."

Next, stick with one issue at a time, and stay in the present tense. Avoid generalizing or predicting the future, such as saying, "You always do this!" If the wife is upset about the husband's purchase of a car without consulting her, she shouldn't start airing her grievance by listing all past transgressions and saying she's come to expect it. That would unfairly indict the other person, overwhelm him with too many examples, and set up a dynamic where he's going to become defensive, Roth says.

Effective communication includes honoring the rule that only one person can talk at a time. "The technique is called mirroring," Roth says. "When the other person talks, restate, as clearly and carefully as possible, what the person says to you. Preface it with, 'I understand' or, 'I see.'"

> When couples work together and resolve issues successfully, they feel good about their relationship, and they receive positive reinforcement and want to do it again!
> — Kristy Archuleta, marriage and family therapist

Avoid name-calling, voice raising, sarcasm, ultimatum giving, or browbeating when talking to your partner. You're trying to foster open communication. "Unloading on the other person is like poison ivy," Roth says. "It feels good to scratch—to let them have it—but the bad condition can spread."

Good communication also requires that each partner give close, full, and respectful attention to the responses of the other. You're asking for your partner's undivided attention and understanding of your thinking process, and from that, your feelings. You must reciprocate. "It's not about agreement, it's about understanding why the other person is thinking one way, and feeling one way," Roth says.

Clearly tell your partner what you agree with from his or her statements, and say what you disagree with.

And, be ready to negotiate. "Try to understand what's really important for your partner," Roth says. "A healthy relationship is built on flexibility. Just because something's important to you doesn't mean it's important to your partner and vice versa. You may decide to agree to disagree and simply accept that you will tolerate an aspect of your partner that is displeasing. For example, your husband may be splurging on green fees because of his golfing hobby. As long as that is his one excessive expenditure and doesn't break the budget, you will put up with it. In exchange, he won't complain about your yoga studio membership." (One solution is the His and Her account setups, discussed in Chapter 11.)

Good communication means that you stay positive. Look for a positive way you've resolved a problem in your relationship or with someone else in the past and apply this method to the current situation.

Make a List and Avoid Relationship Dances

Here's one more strategy to prevent simmering emotions from eventually boiling over into shouting matches. Partners can write lists of what's bothering them, and present them to each other with the agreement that they're committed to solving the problems by talking them out.

The different needs of men and women are especially evident when it comes to investing. Just as men tend not to like asking for directions when traveling, they don't like being told what to do, period. They hate losing, including on investments, and seek ways to redeem themselves. They are less open to guidance than women. In a conflict over investing, women need to take care when broaching the need for counsel with their male mates. Instead of pointing a finger and telling the man he doesn't know what the heck he's doing and already has lost a bundle, she could take the positive-reinforcement tack, saying, for example: "Darling, I love you. But I want to consult a financial planner. I could get a bigger picture of our options, so I can help us better decide to choose investments that will have lower risks and higher returns."

The good news is that when a couple works together and resolves an issue, a sense of accomplishment results.

"When couples work together and resolve issues successfully, they feel good about their relationship, and they receive positive reinforcement and want to do it again!" says marriage therapist Kristy Archuleta. "Couples should look for what works well for them in their relationship, rather than focus on the negative."

Roth cautions partners to be aware of the relationship dances they perform with each other.

If one partner, say the wife, gets worried about money, she might express her stress out loud: "Hey, I'm really scared about how we're going to pay the mortgage next month." But the husband's tendency might be to act calm in the face of pressure. "Don't worry, I've got it under control," he might say.

This may only serve to upset her more and intensify her need to vocalize her fear. He, in turn, may try even harder to reassure her. They end up in a big argument.

"If your partner, the woman in this example, is concerned about something, what might be helpful is for the husband to share in that concern instead of downplaying it," Roth says. "But it's also important for her to know that the louder and more upset she is, she's probably going to make him try to be more calming."

"Success in marriage is much more than finding the right person; it is a matter of being the right person."
—Anonymous

16
The Tasks and Tallies of Divorce

GETTING DIVORCED is time consuming, energy draining, emotionally exhausting, and expensive. Even in the best of circumstances, when the split is relatively amicable, dissolving a marriage is an extended migraine.

Most people who marry for the first time only consider the harsh realities of divorce when they come face to face with the distinct possibility that their marriage could end. Far better to contemplate the misery of divorce *before* getting married. That way, a person will be doubly or triply sure to analyze the merits of marrying his or her partner before proceeding into matrimony.

On a psychological level, experts compare a divorce to losing a loved one to death; the grieving process can take two years. On a financial level, divorce can prove devastating. All the time and effort you two have expended in building up savings and investments, and owning a home, vehicles, and other big-ticket possessions can be subverted by the necessity to divide and liquidate assets. Consider just the home: If it took both your incomes and/or efforts to finance and maintain it, a divorce can mean the home no longer is affordable or feasible for either of you, and it may have to be sold below market value or during a down market for less of a return.

The Realities of the Divorce Process

There are a great many financial and legal realities of the divorce process, which also are strong reasons to think very carefully about how financially compatible you and your partner truly are before you take the plunge into marriage.

You'll need a lawyer—and that costs money. Even with do-it-yourself kits

103

for obtaining a no-fault divorce in a cordial split, you'll still want to consult with a lawyer to ensure the divorce meets court requirements and affords you a just settlement. The issues are too complex to competently handle alone—and especially in the mental fog that afflicts many, if not most, people enduring a divorce. A marital settlement agreement will classify, value, and distribute property, determine spousal and/or child support, and specify child custody and visitation. Avoid proving the truth of the saying, "A man who is his own lawyer has a fool for a client."

Staffers at self-help centers aren't lawyers and can't give legal advice; they can only help people fill out forms. Therefore, you'll have to do the legwork of finding a good divorce lawyer. Ask around to find one who is highly recommended.

Hourly rates for family-law attorneys range from $150 to $750 an hour. The norm in most cities is $250 to $300. If you are pursuing an uncontested divorce, you may end up paying about $1,200 to $1,500 for a lawyer's consultations and several hundred dollars more for the court costs of filing and serving motions.

If your case is contested or complicated, you may pay a great deal more in legal fees. You'll need to retain a lawyer—and that means paying a retainer in advance, which can range from $1,000 to $50,000. The typical range is $2,500 to $5,000. Normally, a lawyer will refund payment for unused hours of the retainer after the case concludes. Read retainer agreements closely.

You'll have to dig up a mountain of paperwork. Unless your divorce is uncontested and unusually amicable, to prepare the marital settlement agreement to the satisfaction of each of your lawyers, you'll each have to round up tax returns, payroll stubs, bank and credit-card statements, property appraisals, pensions, deeds, investments, insurance policies, and business records if either of you owns a business.

You may lose money on investments. In divvying up assets, you may have to liquidate certain investments. This could involve transaction fees and penalties (such as with an early withdrawal of retirement funds). A common scenario is when the partners own a home together, the settlement calls for ownership to go to one of the partners. The other's name must be removed from the title, and that involves a refinancing expense.

A co-owned business will need an appraisal. You'll have to hire a certified business appraiser. A family-owned business is especially difficult to value and divide as an asset. Issues include whether it was established before the marriage, whether it grew substantially after the marriage, whether the growth was due to a spouse not working full-time in the business, whether any separate property of either spouse was invested in the business, and whether both partners run the business as a joint enterprise. If any part of the business is to be considered marital property, this part must be valued—and that involves calculating the worth of hard assets (such as buildings, inventory, and supplies), and the business's goodwill—its value above and beyond the tangible assets, such as its longevity and customer base.

You may have to sell the business. If each spouse was heavily involved in running the business, and you can't remain business partners after the divorce, you may have to sell the business—forfeiting all the toil and trouble, and money you invested in it.

You may need a detective. If you suspect your spouse is hiding assets, you may need to hire a private investigator or forensic accountant. Hidden assets could be anything from stocks and bonds to real estate and hidden bank accounts, motorcycles or boats, or other valuables. A devious spouse can transfer assets to a family member or friend, forcing the lawyer for the other spouse to prove that the transfer was made to deprive the first spouse. Spouses also can claim phony debts. If he or she owns a business, the books could be cooked to obscure assets and make expenses seem higher than they truly are.

> Marriage, divorce, and death of a loved one are three of the largest impacts of stress on a person. The consequence they don't expect is the physical. They're not sleeping, they're not eating, they have high blood pressure, skin issues, inflammation where they can't bend their legs, digestive problems. They don't think clearly when they're not rested or not eating, and therefore they engage in stupid behavior.
> —Marilyn York, divorce lawyer

You'll have to review each piece of property. You'll need to identify which property is clearly owned by which partner separately and which is jointly owned. If you can't come to agreement on everything, you may have to negotiate through lawyers or use a mediator.

Homeowners will need an appraisal. Assuming you jointly own the home you live in, it will have to be appraised at current market value. Unless your relationship is outside the norm, one of you will be leaving this home and perhaps giving up ownership in it. (The spouse awarded primary custody of the children usually remains in the house with the children, unless the spouse can't afford to keep the house.)

You'll have to address the home deed. If you move out of the home but your name remains on the deed, you may unexpectedly end up liable for capital-gains taxes at some point when the home is sold. (No one wants the Internal Revenue Service as your creditor.)

You may have to sell the home. If the value of the home is included in the divvying up of assets, and one spouse gets ownership, this spouse may not be able to continue affording mortgage payments or other costs such as taxes and utilities. (If the homeowner is ordered by the court to pay child support and/or spousal support, these required payments are paramount and are set according to formulas, regardless of whether the payer has a mortgage payment.) In a similar scenario, each spouse may agree before the divorce that the home must be sold. Unless the divorce somehow is timed to the state of the local housing market, the home may end up being sold at an inopportune time.

You'll have to substantiate the debts owed by each spouse. These must be classified the same way as property as either separate property or marital property. What complicates this is that a property-settlement agreement covers only the relationship between spouses; it is not binding on creditors. That means, for example, that if a couple has a car purchased in both their names, it matters not to the lender if the divorce decree says one spouse will get the car and be solely responsible for payment on the loan. If that spouse doesn't pay or goes bankrupt, the lender legally can seek payment from the other spouse.

In a contested divorce, the issue of marital waste can come into play and force one partner to financially reimburse the other partner. The law provides that a spouse has a fiduciary duty toward the other. So, for example, if one partner squandered money on alcohol, drugs, gambling, an expensive trip for himself or herself, spent extravagantly on cosmetic surgery, bought expensive gifts for an extramarital lover, the court may find that this partner must undo his or her financial wrongs by reimbursing the other partner. But the other partner must document this marital waste.

You may be liable for credit debt run up by your spouse. If you've jointly signed with your partner on loans or credit cards, you'll be liable for debts on these accounts—including those your partner racks up after you've begun pursuing the divorce. So you must notify each lender in writing that you will not be responsible for any more debts on the account above the present outstanding balance. The family court cannot protect you against creditor liability. Creditors won't release you just because you've gotten divorced.

You may have to protect your credit score. If your ex-spouse defaults on a marital debt that he or she had agreed to pay, this can negatively affect your own credit score. So you are advised to negotiate new credit terms in a separate agreement with each of your creditors. But there's no guarantee a creditor will agree to refinance a debt in your name alone.

You may face an IRS audit. You'll need to decide how to handle any possible audit of jointly filed income-tax returns. If the IRS finds an alleged deficiency, will the spouse who underreported his or her income, or took too many deductions, make good on this tax debt? Your defense, if your spouse is guilty of this false reporting, can be that you were clueless—an innocent spouse. However, sometimes the family court holds a spouse accountable for debt owed to the IRS as a result of an audit because that spouse benefited from the income—even if the spouse didn't know the extent to which income had been underreported. A tax lawyer should be hired if you receive a deficiency notice from the IRS. If you co-owned a business and one partner retains the business after the divorce, this partner should agree to indemnify the other partner from corporate or personal tax liability.

You'll need to protect your personal assets. This means moving cash and investments into your own accounts separate from your spouse. But it also means safeguarding your personal belongings. The initial separation can be the most emotional and vindictive phase of the divorce process. Lawyers have seen angry spouses steal or destroy their partners' irreplaceable valuables such as jewelry, heirlooms, collectibles—and even photographs of deceased loved ones. Veteran divorce lawyer Marilyn York advises, "Get your invaluable possessions somewhere safe first. These are the items that you would take if your home was on fire."

You'll need to remove your ex-spouse's name from key documents. These include as your beneficiary in your will and on insurance polices and retirement plans. You'll have to wait until after the divorce is final to change your will because a disinherited spouse can contest a new will as long as the two of you are married.

You may need to get new insurance coverage. If you were covered by your spouse's insurance plan through his or her employer, you may have to get new coverage. The federal law known as COBRA allows a former spouse of a divorced person who is working for a company with 20 or more people and who is a participant in that employer's medical plan, to remain on that insurance plan for up to 36 months following the divorce. But you will have to pay for the coverage yourself.

You'll need to address powers of attorney. You'll have to destroy any power of attorney that gives your partner control over your assets or health decisions. A written revocation is probably the safest method.

You may want to legally change your name. For example, if you're a woman who took on her husband's last name, you may want to return to your previous last name.

You may want to change your name on legal documents. These include on your financial accounts, business documents, driver's license, Social Security card, and passport.

You may have to pay alimony. Alimony, also known as spousal support, may be required by the court even during the pending divorce. This is ordinarily tax deductible for the spouse who pays it and is taxed as income by the spouse who receives it. If you declare bankruptcy, you'll still have to pay alimony, although you can try to have the family court adjust the payments.

You may have to pay child support. This is not tax deductible for the spouse who pays it (but is not taxed as income by the spouse who receives it). Failure to pay child support can result in garnished wages, intercepted tax refunds, and even jail. As with alimony, declaring bankruptcy won't relieve you of the requirement of making child-support payments, although you can ask the court to adjust the payments. Divorce lawyer Marilyn York notes: "The first thing the district attorney can do in California and Nevada if you owe more than $1,000 in child support or alimony is suspend your driver's license and/ or revoke your passport."

You may have to battle over who keeps the cat or dog. If you own pets, ownership will have to be determined by the partners. An agreement can be included in the property-settlement agreement filed with the court. In extreme cases, couples choose shared custody or visitation. "The court will do a dog-custody battle," York says. "Some courts treat pets as property, like a couch, and some courts deal with them as living beings and consider what is in the best interest of the pet. It can become a big nasty issue, particularly with people with no kids and who are huge pet lovers."

You'll have to spend considerable time tying up loose ends. This includes informing numerous parties of the terms of the property settlement after it is finalized—insurance agents, stockbrokers, bankers, accountants, pension-fund administrators, and anyone else involved with your financial affairs.

You'll miss time from work. "When you're going through the divorce, it's a substantial time commitment," York says. "You have to let your employer know you'll miss work hours. Court proceedings are for appointments during the workday, not during evening or weekend hours. And there are depositions and the pulling of paperwork."

If you have children, you'll have to spend daytime hours visiting schools and determining where your child is going to be attending. And finding new living arrangements also may be a daytime chore.

Side-effects May Include Heartburn, Insomnia, and Stupid Behavior

Recovering emotionally from a divorce can be like working through the stages of grief over the death of a loved one or recovery from Post-Traumatic Stress Disorder. There's shock and denial, anger and resentment, bargaining (trying to reconcile), depression, and—finally—acceptance. The process can unfold slowly over time, and the phases can transpire in different orders with reversals.

Divorce lawyer York says women tend to mourn the demise of a relationship while still in it. Therefore, women often are more ready to move on. "Men tend to be blindsided," York says. "They'll say, 'This is completely out of nowhere.'"

However, each person is different. Many variables come into play for the length of recovering psychologically from a divorce. These include the length of the marriage, the circumstances that triggered the divorce (a spouse's infidelity seems to affect women more than the divorce itself, York says), the economic devastation in the aftermath, and whether children are involved.

"Typically if the financial settlement was fair or once a person is financially out of the hole, the person is over the divorce," York says. But if there's a custody battle over a child or children, a parent won't get over the divorce until he or she gains the desired degree of custody. If that isn't achieved, the divorce trauma can persist even for the rest of the person's life.

Divorces typically impact more than just the two spouses. "Everyone around you is sucked into this," York says. "It can take down three generations of a family: the couple, their children, and also the couple's parents because they're usually the first people a divorced person goes to for financial assistance."

No matter how amicable a divorce, the process involves a measure of conflict. "Some people can handle conflict, and some can't," York says. "Some people relish conflict. They like it. Others get physically sick. Some have heart attacks or kill themselves because of divorces. People need never to underestimate the impact divorce can have on them—emotionally and physically as well as financially.

"Marriage, divorce, and death of a loved one are three of the largest impacts of stress on a person. The consequence they don't expect is the physical. I've seen this over and over with clients: They're not sleeping, they're not eating, they have high blood pressure, skin issues, inflammation where they can't bend their legs, digestive problems. They can't work as much, and they're nervous about being broker than ever, and not being able to spend the night with their kids. They don't think clearly when they're not rested or not eating, and therefore they engage in stupid behavior."

York says that people going through divorce can benefit greatly from counseling. If they are parents, they should consider co-parenting therapists. These professionals can teach ex-spouses how to parent their children under the new circumstances. Co-parenting therapists can even benefit nonparents, York says. A couple getting divorced may need to divide pets or a business. "There is a specific set of skills you can learn to separate assets in a less traumatic way," York says.

People going through divorce should understand that they'll not be thinking or acting like their normal selves. "Criminal attorneys have a saying that they 'see bad people at their best,'" York says. "The famous saying by divorce lawyers is, 'You see good people at their worst.'"

Conclusion

FOR A marriage to succeed, it takes work by each partner. It demands continued commitment, compromise, and sacrifice. A great many couples find this challenge too difficult or too undesirable to see it through. Others manage to honor their marital vows until death, not debt, do them part.

The institution of marriage has proved a fertile ground for humor throughout the ages. "Keep your eyes wide open before marriage, and half-shut afterwards," Benjamin Franklin recommended. The merit of the second part of his witticism is debatable. The first part, however, is sage advice, especially when it comes to assessing whether you and your partner are a money match.

The best method of preventing financial issues from developing into irreconcilable differences during a marriage is to openly and thoroughly address those issues—including before marriage.

A Scottish saying goes: "Don't marry for money. You can borrow it cheaper."

How true, given the toll a divorce can exact.

The late English comedian Bob Monkhouse quipped: "Marriage is an investment which pays dividends if you pay interest."

How true, again.

Hopefully, this book will help every reader considering marriage to pay the proper interest to an area that often determines whether the union will fail or succeed. That area is *financial compatibility*.

Here's hoping you and your partner will prove to be a good money match if the two of you decide to invest together in that age-old, sacred institution known as matrimony.

List of Personal-finance Books

HERE IS a list of some of the books on personal finance that the American Institute for Economic Research offers at reasonable prices (generally $8 to $12). You can survey and order these titles online at www.aier.org/bookstore, or by calling toll free: (888) 528-1216.

The Estate Plan Book

How to Avoid Financial Tangles

How to Invest Wisely

How to Plan for Your Retirement Years

How to Build Wealth With Tax-Sheltered Investments

Start Here: Getting Your Financial Life on Track

What You Need to Know about Mutual Funds

What Your Car Really Costs

Appendix: Wedding Costs

A WEDDING can be an expensive venture. The worksheet below provides a breakdown of the many costs that can be associated with a such an event. It's a good budget tool that can help couples see both the big picture cost and the expenditure details.

Your total budget $_____

Item	Amount budgeted	Vendor estimate	Amount spent
Reception (40 percent)			
Venue and rentals (tables, etc.)			
Food and service			
Beverages (including bartenders)			
Cake			
Security			
Guestbook			
Rice/rose petals/bubbles			
Child care			
Miscellaneous fees			

Reception total $_____

Item	Amount budgeted	Vendor estimate	Amount spent
Apparel (10 percent)			
Bride's gown (and alterations)			
Bride's headpiece and veil			
Bride's shoes			
Bride's accessories			
Bride's hair and makeup			
Bridesmaids' dresses			
Bridesmaids' shoes			
Bridesmaids' accessories			
Groom's accessories			
Groom's tuxedo or suit			
Groomsmen's tuxedos or suits			
Garters			
Going-away outfit			
Honeymoon clothes			

Apparel total $_____

Item	Amount budgeted	Vendor estimate	Amount spent
Flowers, decor (10 percent)			
Altarpiece			
Floral arrangements for ceremony			
Flower girl's buds and basket			
Bride's bouquet			
Bridesmaids' bouquets			
Throwaway bouquet			
Boutonniere			
Corsages			
Ring pillow			
Reception decorations			
Lighting			
Miscellaneous fees			

Flowers/Decor total $_____

Item	Amount budgeted	Vendor estimate	Amount spent
Music (10 percent)			
Music for rehearsal dinner			
Musicians for ceremony			
Cocktail-hour musicians			
Band or DJ for reception			
Sound-system rental			
Dance-floor fee/rentals			
Miscellaneous fees			

Music total $_____

Item	Amount budgeted	Vendor estimate	Amount spent
Photography (10 percent)			
Engagement photos			
Bridal portraits			
Ceremony photography			
Reception photography			
Videography			
Additional prints/albums			
Miscellaneous fees			

Photography total $_____

Item	Amount budgeted	Vendor estimate	Amount spent
Rehearsal dinner (10 percent)			
Beverages (including bartender)			
Food and service			
Venue and rentals (tables, etc.)			
Parking (valet)			
Miscellaneous fees			

Rehearsal dinner total $_____

Item	Amount budgeted	Vendor estimate	Amount spent
Gifts/favors (3 percent)			
Bridal-party gifts			
Gifts to out-of-town guests			
Reception favors for guests			
Miscellaneous fees			

Gifts/favors dinner total $_____

Item	Amount budgeted	Vendor estimate	Amount spent
Ceremony (2 percent)			
Site fee (or donation)			
Officiant fee			
Ushers			
Guestbook/pen			
Child care			
Miscellaneous fees			

Ceremony total $_____

Item	Amount budgeted	Vendor estimate	Amount spent
Wedding rings (2 percent)			
Engagement ring			
Bride's wedding ring			
Groom's wedding ring			

Wedding rings $_____

Item	Amount budgeted	Vendor estimate	Amount spent
Stationery (2 percent)			
Newspaper announcement			
Bachelor-party invitations			
Bridesmaid luncheon invitations			
Save-the-date cards			
Invitations/RSVP cards			
Map/direction cards			
Seating and place cards			
Menu cards			
Thank-you cards			
Postage			
Miscellaneous fees			

Stationery total $_____

Item	Amount budgeted	Vendor estimate	Amount spent
Transportation (1 percent)			
Limo/car rental for bride, groom			
Limo/car rental for bridal party			
Transport for out-of-town guests			
Ceremony parking (valet)			
Reception parking (valet)			
Miscellaneous fees			

Transportation total $_____

You may also want to factor in your honeymoon budget:

Item	Amount budgeted	Vendor estimate	Amount spent
Honeymoon			
Airfare			
Accommodations			
Rental car			
Entertainment			
Miscellaneous fees			

Honeymoon total $_____

Finally, if you do use a wedding planner, factor in the fee:

Planner fee $_____

Index

The Benefits of
AIER MEMBERSHIP

If you found this book helpful, you'll also benefit from AIER's newsletters. Our timely articles offer valuable insight on important economic and personal finance issues.

Our twice-monthly *Research Reports* provide concise discussion concerning a wide range of current issues. One article each month is devoted to deciphering where we are in the business cycle.

Our monthly *Economic Bulletin* presents in-depth treatment of topics pertaining to economics, fiscal policy, retirement, and personal finance.

Once you become a member you will also receive 50% off all AIER books. Support our educational efforts by becoming an AIER member today. Print and digital memberships now available.

Call us toll-free: (888) 528-1216

Visit us online: www.aier.org